Draw MANGA

RUTH KEATTCH

hinkler

hinkler

© Hinkler Pty Ltd 2023
45–55 Fairchild Street
Heatherton Victoria 3202 Australia
www.hinkler.com

Author and illustrator: Ruth Keattch
Cover design: Ben Sanders
Design and editorial: Tall Tree Limited

Images © Hinkler Pty Ltd or Shutterstock

ISBN: 978 1 4889 5406 1

Printed and bound in China

CONTENTS

WHAT IS MANGA?

Manga refers to a style of comics or graphic novels that originally came from Japan. Most manga conform to ever-evolving styles that began in the 1960s with such titles as *Astroboy*. A little-known fact about manga is that while the style has its origins in woodblock printing (called ukiyo-e), the large eyes of manga were influenced by the look of early Disney films like *Snow White and the Seven Dwarfs*. Outside Japan, the word is typically used to refer to comics originally published in Japan, although there are other forms of manga that come from China and South Korea, called manhua and manhwa respectively.

In Japan, people of all ages and walks of life read manga. The medium includes works in a broad range of genres: action, adventure, comedy, detective, drama, historical, horror, mystery, romance, science fiction and fantasy, sports and games, suspense, and many others! The number of genres will continue to grow as manga's popularity around the world increases.

Manga is widely enjoyed across the globe, and you will find it in many mainstream bookstores and libraries today. It is usually drawn by a single mangaka (manga artist) who works with a small team. This is the case for larger titles like *One Piece, Berserk* and *My Hero Academia*. As a small creator you won't have your own team for a while, so be prepared for a lot of hard work – but you will find all the tools you need to succeed within the pages of *Unbinders Draw Manga*!

MATERIALS

TO GET STARTED

You will need some simple tools to get started on your manga journey. The first place to start is with pencils and paper. You can then use fineliners to help you refine and finalise your manga drawings.

PENCILS

Initially, good-quality pencils are all you need for drawing manga. Pencils come in different grades. Each artist is different and has their own preferences. However, to get started, it's recommended you work with a soft graphite pencil type – HB or 2B are ideal choices. These are also available as mechanical pencils, which are a common choice for mangaka.

PAPER

Choosing the right paper is also important when starting out – look for a hard-wearing paper that can withstand the use of an eraser on its surface. Avoid thin paper like printer paper, and invest in a decent sketchbook with a paper weight of at least 100gsm. This won't tear if you need to use an eraser and it also won't allow the ink to bleed into the fibres when you come to ink your work.

FINELINER PENS

Fineliners come in many different weights and widths and can be confusing at first glance. However, the number on the top of the lid and on the label will tell you the weight of the pen. The smaller the number, the thinner the stroke, so keep this in mind when selecting your ink pens. It's normal to have a range of weights and sizes; for the smaller details, a 0.1 fineliner is a good starting weight, while a 0.5 is better for thicker lines.

THE BASICS

THE BASICS

All skills begin with the basics! In this chapter we are going to cover the fundamentals of drawing to help you get started on your manga journey.

BASIC MANGA SHAPES

In all styles of drawing, it's important to get the shape and composition right. Certain shapes will help you to understand the form of human bodies, landscapes, objects and animals. Practising these shapes will give you the confidence to master your illustration skills and lead to you tackling more complicated designs.

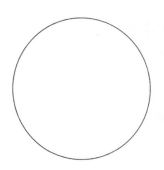

CIRCLES

Circles form the basis of many elements in manga, from heads to joints. We use circles to help us map out perspectives and to ensure that angles are correct in our compositions.

CONNECTORS

Circles are connected with lines – this is the basis of limbs and wireframes (see pages 18–19).

RECTANGLES

Rectangles help us flesh out the connectors into solid objects. Here, you can see how using these simple shapes can be the starting point for all your sketches. These three shapes in combination will make up the majority of your compositions, and learning how they fit together will help you advance quickly. It may seem counterproductive to spend time practising these shapes, but the faster you become familiar with them the easier you will find it to advance, so practise, practise, practise!

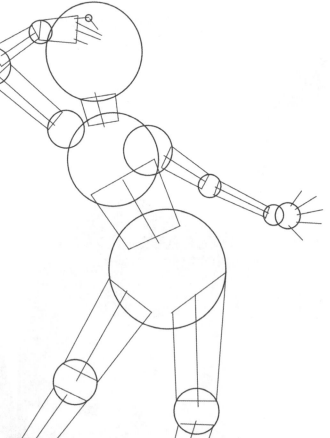

THE HEAD AND FACE

Heads and faces are some of the most important elements of the human body to get right – they play a key role in injecting expression into your work and give your characters their personality and individuality.

1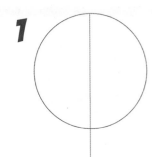
Draw a circle then add a line down the centre extending out from the base of the circle – this line is your midpoint, which you will use to plot the rest of the face.

2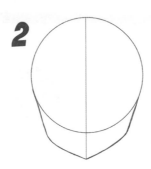
Draw an upside-down tent shape for the chin. This is the most-common face shape in manga and will give your drawing an authentic feel.

3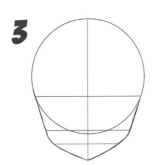
Draw a line across the circle as shown – this is the eyeline. Halfway between the eyeline and chin, add another line for the location of the nose. Place another line halfway between the nose and the chin for the mouth line.

4
The eyes sit on the eyeline an equal width apart. The width of the eyes should be the same as the distance between them. The ears are roughly the same size as the eyes and should be placed at the same level.

5
Younger face

The age of your character affects the shape of the facial features. Younger children have large eyes and small features (left), while adults have smaller eyes and a more refined face shape.

6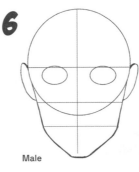
Male

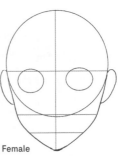
Female

You can show female faces by drawing larger eyes and a softer jawline, and male faces with smaller eyes and a stronger jawline.

9

MANGA EYES

Manga eyes are varied and are usually oversized and super expressive – the eyes are the windows to the soul after all! It's worth taking the time to get this right as the eyes can affect the overall look of your characters and make all the difference between a successful drawing and one you're less happy with.

1 Start off with a simplified eye shape. Manga eyes are similar in shape to real eyes, so referring to images of real faces might be helpful when sketching out your ideas.

Realistic

Simplified

2 Once you have a simplified eye you need to determine which parts should be developed to turn it into a manga-style eye. Add definition to the upper and lower lash lines. Next, draw a circle between the two lash lines for the iris, with a light reflection at the bottom.

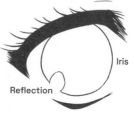
Iris
Reflection
Manga-style

3 To add detail to the eyes, draw a thicker line around the iris. Shade the pupil in the middle, adding a further light reflection. Once you have drawn this neutral eye you can experiment with different expressions (see page 14).

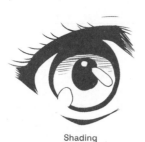
Shading

Gather some inspiration for different eye styles from this selection.

THE NOSE AND MOUTH

The next step in creating a manga character's face is to draw the nose and mouth. Although the nose can be a simple triangle shape, it's worth experimenting to find a shape that works for your character. The mouth can reveal a lot about a personality and their emotions. Here are some ideas to spark your imagination.

1 Noses are simplified in manga, so avoid over-detailing the nostrils. Here is a simple nose with some options for alternative nose shapes shown to the right.

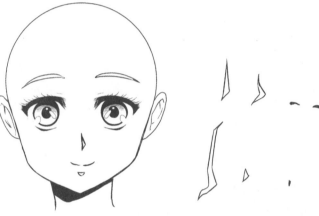

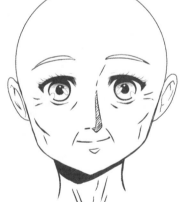

2 To create older characters, you can add more definition to the facial features, including nostrils and wrinkle lines. The opposite is true for younger faces – a dot can be enough or you can leave out the nose altogether!

3 The mouth can be drawn as a single curved line. Mouths are rarely, if ever, perfectly straight, so stick to curved lines. With age, the mouth changes shape and introducing definition to the lips will help you draw an older character. When drawing an open mouth, keep it in proportion with the rest of the face to make sure the mouth doesn't appear abnormally large.

EARS AND NECK

Ears can be difficult to sketch out, so a good first point of reference is to check the shape of your own ears in a mirror! In terms of placement, the ears are always in line with the eyes, and are roughly the same size or larger. When filling in the detail of the ears, pay careful attention to the structure and avoid oversimplification.

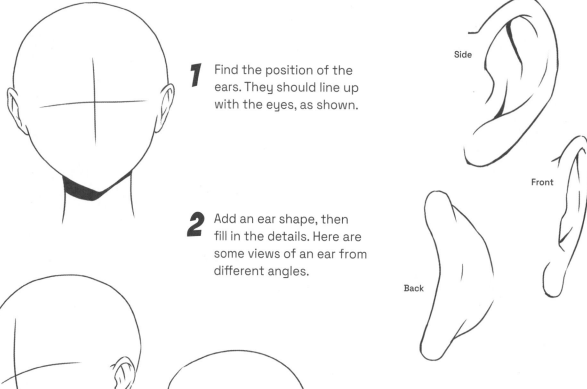

1 Find the position of the ears. They should line up with the eyes, as shown.

2 Add an ear shape, then fill in the details. Here are some views of an ear from different angles.

Side

Front

Back

3 The neck comes down from the base of the head using curved lines. The shape of these lines changes with the angle of the head. For example, if you are looking from the side you'll see a smooth curve from the back of the neck downwards. You can also vary the width, with male characters having thicker necks and children's necks being much narrower and shorter.

SKETCHING A BUST

Now it's time to put some elements together – head, neck, shoulders and bust. This will help you to construct the overall shape of the upper body. References are useful here! If you are struggling to visualise the shape, look at your own features in a mirror, or find images online.

1 Here you can see how male and female body shapes can be formed. Construct the upper torso using the circles and connectors mentioned on page 8.

Male

Female

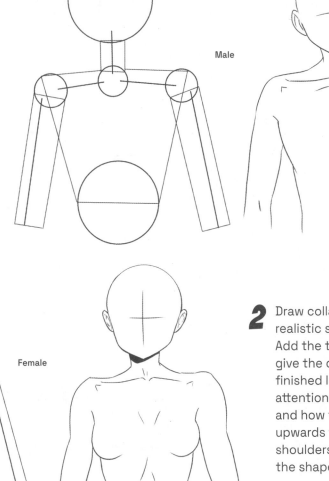

2 Draw collarbones to add a realistic shape to the body. Add the tops of the arms to give the character a more finished look. Pay particular attention to the collarbones and how they curve upwards towards the shoulders, connecting the shape together.

FACIAL EXPRESSIONS

Now that you have drawn manga-style face shapes, eyes and mouths, it's time to add these elements together to create visual expressions. These will allow your character to show emotion.

HAPPY

The eyes should be open, with an upwards curve. Characters can beam with so much happiness that they close their eyes too, with big open mouths. The eyebrows can be open, wide and curved to frame the eyes.

ANGRY

The eyebrows play a prominent role in this expression. They are curved downwards, obscuring the eyes slightly. Make the teeth clenched, and add some wrinkles on the forehead to show tension in the face.

SAD

The eyes can be teary, with small circles on the lower lash line to emulate tears. You can add a frown and eyebrows that are angled upwards in concern.

CONFUSED

A single raised eyebrow easily conveys this expression, with a neutral expression on the lips.

EMBARRASSED

To show embarrassment, draw lines across the face to simulate the blush that this emotion causes.

HANDS AND FEET

Hands and feet can be tricky. Look at your own hands and you'll notice that the palm itself, while mostly square when flat, curves like a shovel when it's in action, so take care to show this in your work.

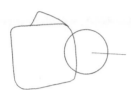

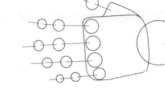

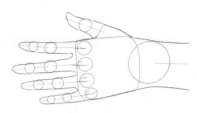

1 For the hands, start with the shape of the palm, which resembles a rounded square. Sketch in a small triangle on one side to create the space where the thumb will protrude from the hand. Add a circle and line for the wrist joint.

2 Looking at your fingers, the pinky finger is the smallest, and the middle is the longest. Along one edge of the curved square draw circles to represent the knuckles. Draw two circles for the joints on each finger and join them using connecting lines.

3 Try not to get discouraged at this point – hands are very tricky! Once you have established the composition, begin to flesh out the fingers, using the circles as reference for the thickness of the digits.

4 Erase the circles and lines and add in the details like the nails and outlines of the knuckles.

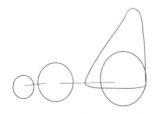

1 Start the foot by drawing a triangle shape. At the base of the triangle draw a circle to represent the heel. Add circles for the pads and joints of the foot and the toes. Join these using connector lines.

2 Complete the toes by rounding off the ends and add an outline to the foot.

3 Flesh out the digits then erase your guidelines and add the final details.

HAIR

To get started with your character's hair, you need to establish the hairline. The shape of the hairstyle will start from here and once it's established you can add strands falling over it.

1 Draw a line on the forehead that is about halfway between the character's eyes and the top of the head. This will give you a rough indication of where to place the hairline. Hair grows naturally upwards and out from the scalp. To help you visualise this, imagine that the strands of hair are actually arrows indicating the direction of the hair. The longer the hair, the greater the effect of gravity on its weight, so be sure to curve longer hair downwards.

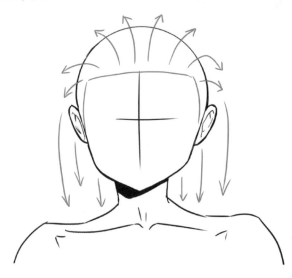

2 While it may be tempting to draw every single strand, manga hair is more commonly drawn in clumps and shapes. Here are a few examples to get you started.

Short, spiky hair – note the pointed shapes.

Long, flowing hair – note the downward direction of the strands.

Shoulder-length curly hair – note that the emphasis is on its overall shape and not the individual strands.

HAIRSTYLING

Once you've decided on the length of the hair, you can think about the hairstyle. Here are some ideas for longer hair.

PLAITS:

Gather the hair to the top of the plait, and draw petal-like shapes in a rope downwards. The petals should overlap slightly to give the impression of the hair being plaited down. Once you have this single 'rope', bulk it out with a second layer to simulate the whole plait.

PONYTAILS:

Gather the hair to the point where the ponytail will begin. Plot the shape of the ponytail – is it straight or curly hair? This will help you to visualise the overall ponytail.

BUNS:

Gather the hair to the point the bun will begin. The process is similar to drawing ponytails, except this time, keep the hair in a rough circular shape.

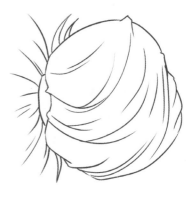

BODY COMPOSITION AND PERSPECTIVE

Wireframes are a simplified way of looking at the body and how it moves. With wireframes you can use your previous understanding of circles and connectors and apply it to the whole body. This will help to improve your understanding of how the body moves, before you add the details.

1 Draw a basic human wireframe like this, which includes the chest, hips, hands, feet and head. Then add lines and circles for the limbs and joints. Circles can be used to represent a joint that can be moved to create angles and compositions.

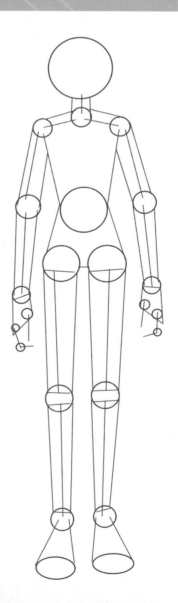

2 Use wireframes when making thumbnail sketches. These are quick sketches used to test out body composition and angles so you can quickly visualise the action you are trying to convey. They should only be about 6 cm (2.4 in) in height – the larger the thumbnail, the longer it is likely to take you to draw. By keeping the sketch small, you'll be able to try out a number of different angles in a short space of time and get one that you're happy with.

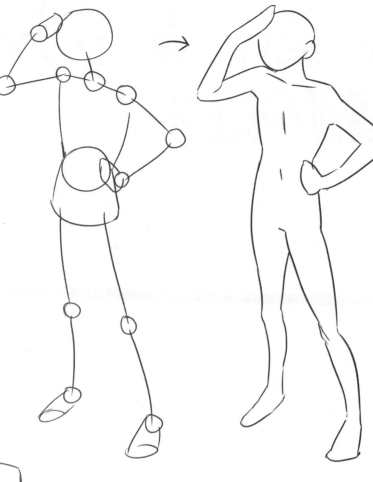

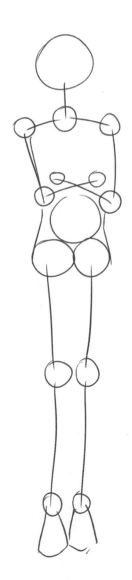

3 When you are happy with a composition, work it up into a larger overall image. Take your wireframe and draw around it, creating what will look like a featureless gingerbread man. Next, add in some details including the belly button, collarbones, muscles (if the muscle shapes are visible), and so on. If you struggle with this, seek out references, either by looking at your own body in a mirror or finding images online.

DRAWING DIFFERENT ANGLES

If you draw manga characters within a story setting, you'll need to show them in a range of different poses, depending on the action in a particular scene. Here are some ideas on how to show your characters in motion.

1 Draw a wireframe, putting your character into a position that you need for your story.

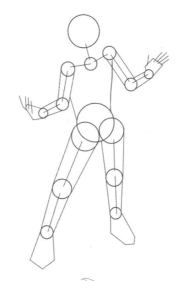
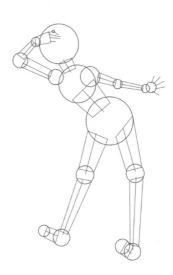

2 Draw around your wireframe using the methods shown on page 19. Then add the details of your character (see page 28).

FORESHORTENING

Foreshortening is the process of creating an illusion of depth or distance in a drawing. It is a useful skill to learn when adding dynamic action to your manga scenes. For example, you may want to show a figure with one arm outstretched towards the viewer or show someone looking up from the ground.

1 Once you've decided the pose you want to show, draw a wireframe figure. Make the parts of the body that are closest to the viewer larger and those further away smaller than they would be if you were drawing a figure straight on without foreshortening. In this case, the left side of the body is facing the viewer so the left leg and arm are larger to make them jump off the page.

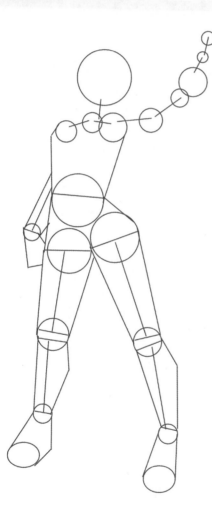

2 Draw around your wireframe using the methods shown on page 19. Then add the details of your character (see page 28).

ADDING CLOTHING

Fabric flows in line with gravity, motion and external effects like the wind. The weight of the fabric affects how it looks – thicker fabrics, like wool, are less affected by the wind, for instance. Drawing fabric alone is only one aspect of showing clothing, as you also need to think about the way fabric gathers and clings around your character's body.

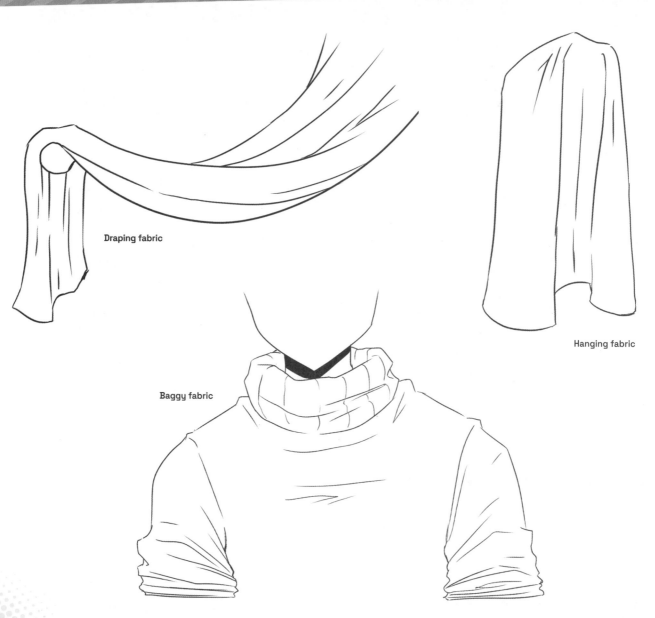

Draping fabric

Hanging fabric

Baggy fabric

GRAVITY PULL

This wrinkle occurs in the fabric when it is flowing downwards.

GATHERED CREASE

These wrinkles are around the joints of the body like the shoulders, elbows and knees.

TENSION PULL

These wrinkles occur when there is a pull effect on them – for example, when a character is stretching or reaching.

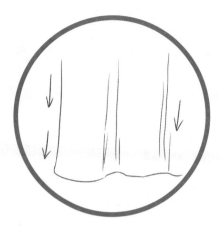

Where the clothing fits around the joints (including the underarms and at the hips), you need to show creases in the fabric to indicate the stresses around those areas. With baggier clothing, there are actually fewer wrinkles, as the fabric does not cling to the body in the same way that tighter clothing does.

As an example, have a look at this character in a simple T-shirt. Here you can see how the fabric is shown as being baggy on the sleeves and tight at the waist.

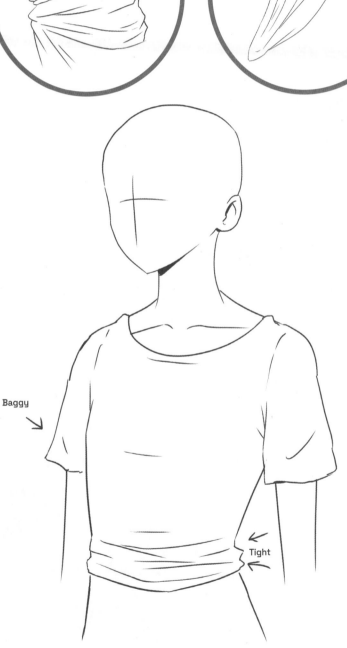

Baggy

Tight

MANGA CLOTHING

Here are a few different styles you may want to consider when picking clothes for your manga characters. Of course, you can choose any clothing that you like that works within your story, but these are some of the archetypes of manga style.

DRESSES AND ROBES

MODERN CLOTHING

TRADITIONAL JAPANESE CLOTHING

FUTURISTIC STYLE

USING PERSPECTIVE

Once you have a manga figure, you'll want to place them in their own world. To create your own backgrounds and environments, you'll need to understand the basics of perspective. This is a way of showing 3D objects on a flat piece of paper. Artists often use 1-, 2- and 3-point perspectives to help map the world around them.

1-POINT PERSPECTIVE

In 1-point perspective, all the vanishing lines of an object meet at a single point in the distance called a vanishing point. Start with a single vanishing point and radiate lines out from it to help you map objects in the scene. This perspective is used to draw room interiors.

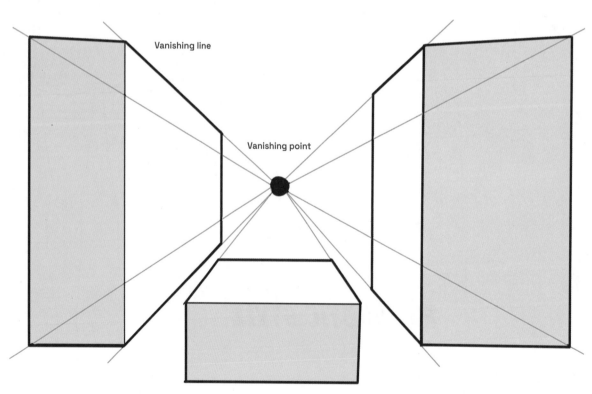

Vanishing line

Vanishing point

2-POINT PERSPECTIVE

This type of perspective has lines that converge on two vanishing points in the distance to create a 3D effect. It can be used for exteriors and buildings. Draw two vanishing points on a horizon line, then from each of those points draw lines downwards to form a cube shape. These lines determine the angles of the cube.

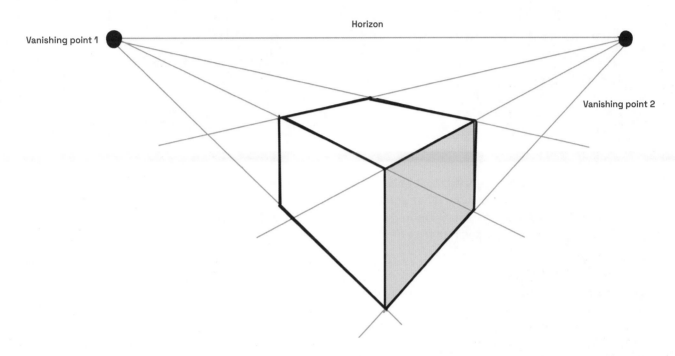

3-POINT PERSPECTIVE

Add a third vanishing point for 3-point perspective. This perspective creates a dynamic composition likened to a fish-eye lens. It's mostly used in action shots and establishing shots. Begin in the same way as for 2-point perspective, with two vanishing points to draw the base of the cube. Then add a third vanishing point either above or below. In this example, the third vanishing point is below so the cube looks as though it's being viewed from above.

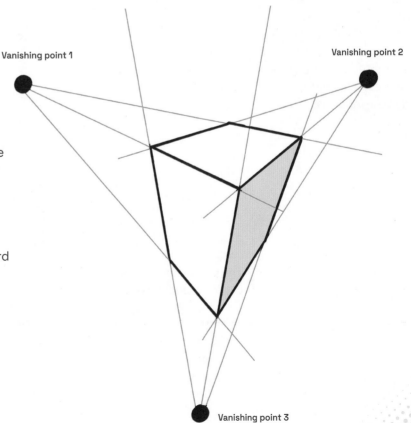

CHARACTER CREATION

Now it's time to add the details. Think about how much detail you want to add – too little and you risk your character appearing boring, but too much and it will be overwhelming for the viewer. Also, by not adding too many details, you'll find it easier to draw the character over and over again.

First, establish your character's basic details – what is their name? How old are they? What gender are they? Second, consider what you want their overall character to be – are they determined? Moody? Caring? Hot-tempered? These questions will help you to add details to your drawing that give the viewer an idea of their personality.

Finally, are there any existing manga characters or styles you already like? Knowing what you enjoy drawing, or aspire to draw, can give you inspiration. On pages 105–115 we will dive into the different genres of manga, which will give you some more ideas for your own characters. Once you've considered all these elements, you can start to sketch your character.

1 Make a head-to-toe map of your character's body shape (see pages 18–19). The body can be in a simple T-pose position, allowing you to add the hairstyle, eyes, clothing, proportions and perspective.

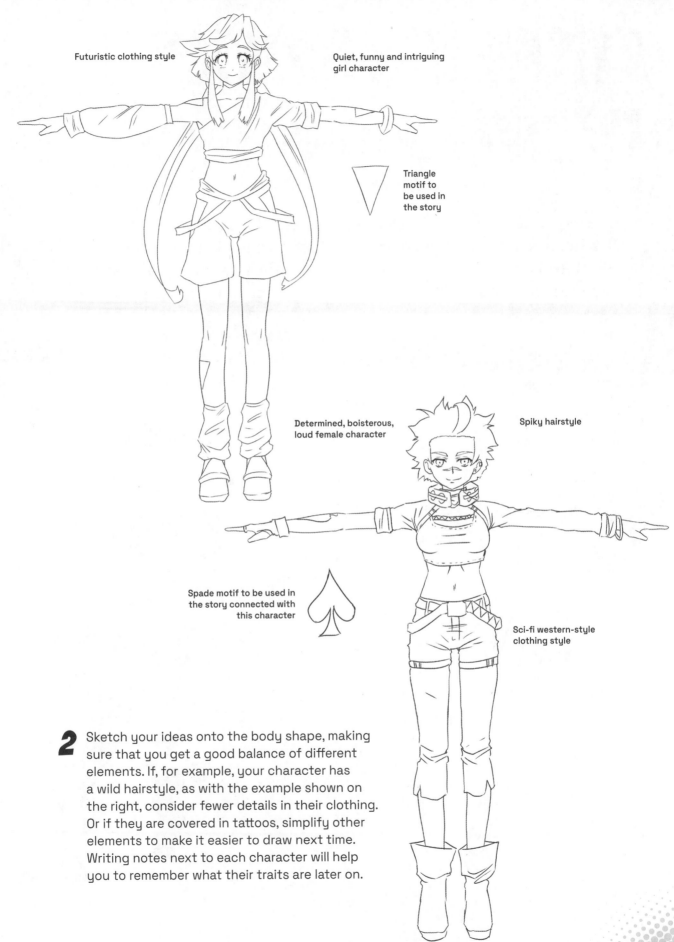

Futuristic clothing style

Quiet, funny and intriguing girl character

Triangle motif to be used in the story

Determined, boisterous, loud female character

Spiky hairstyle

Spade motif to be used in the story connected with this character

Sci-fi western-style clothing style

2 Sketch your ideas onto the body shape, making sure that you get a good balance of different elements. If, for example, your character has a wild hairstyle, as with the example shown on the right, consider fewer details in their clothing. Or if they are covered in tattoos, simplify other elements to make it easier to draw next time. Writing notes next to each character will help you to remember what their traits are later on.

EXAMPLE CHARACTER DRAWING

Here you can see how to develop a character from start to finish. So far, you have learned enough to get to the outline stage. Colour, light and shade are discussed in more depth later on (see pages 68–69), but hopefully this will inspire you to see what's possible!

Wireframe   Outline added   Colour added

FANTASY MANGA

FANTASY MANGA

The fantasy genre is everywhere you look, including manga! Here we will show you how to incorporate this magical theme into your drawings with ease.

FANTASY BASICS: ARMOUR

Armour is essential in any fantasy setting, so it's important to have an idea about different types of armour and how they fit your characters. Armour can be steel plate, chain mail or leather, and can be combined with furs. On this page, you will see a basic steel set of armour, which you can adapt to suit your needs.

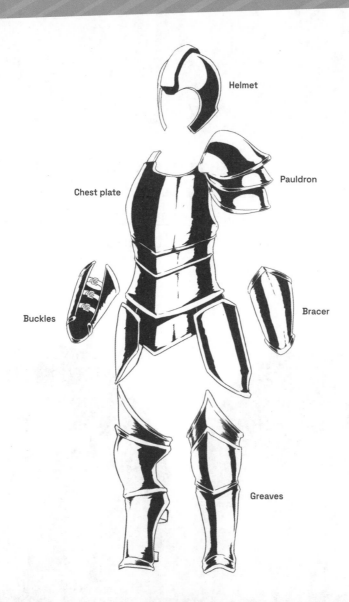

Helmet

Pauldron

Chest plate

Buckles

Bracer

Greaves

CHEST PLATE

This covers the full top half of the body and fits snugly over the torso. Here is one example of a simple chest plate – there are many more types to try depending on the style of your character.

PAULDRONS

The shoulder coverings in a suit of armour are called pauldrons. These can be shown in combination with a chest plate. Pauldrons sit flush with the body shape. There can be many variations of pauldrons – some are spiked and some layered, as here.

BRACERS

Bracers go over the forearms and are usually held in place with buckles. They come in many styles including with spikes, layers and fur. Buckles are an important element of armour. Take a look at a real belt buckle and observe its form to make sure your drawing looks right.

GREAVES

Greaves are similar to bracers, but are positioned over the lower legs.

HELMET

Here you can see how the helmet fits closely to the head. Start by drawing the head as on page 9, then add an outline around that shape to get a realistic look. Finally, add the detail of the helmet.

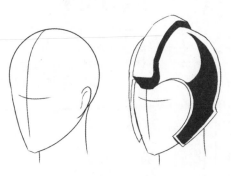

FANTASY BASICS: WEAPONS

Along with armour, weapons are commonly included in fantasy settings. Many of the best-known characters in fantasy fiction and films have weapons that are an integral part of their story, so let's look at some examples.

SWORDS

Swords are the most commonly used weapons in fantasy art. The general form and shape of swords can vary considerably. The basic version is dual edged, meaning it is sharp on both sides, and the most common sword depicted in fantasy manga is usually a broadsword. These typically have a cross bar above the handle protecting the wielder from the sharp blade.

Experiment with this basic shape to give your swords some variation. Adding a curve or thickening or thinning the blade can give it a unique look. There are many different types of sword, so be creative. Here is an idea for a fantasy Japanese sword.

Broadsword

Japanese sword

DAGGERS

The shape and form of a dagger is like that of a sword, but with a shorter blade. You can design your own variations by altering the shape of the blade and the handle and adding decoration.

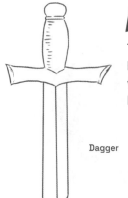

Dagger

BOW

The bow is a classic fantasy weapon often wielded by elves and rangers. The basic shape of a bow is one curved piece with a single string connecting the tips. When the bow is drawn, the curve of the bow deepens. When designing a bow, add a place in the centre for a hand to hold it. Try different variations around these common elements.

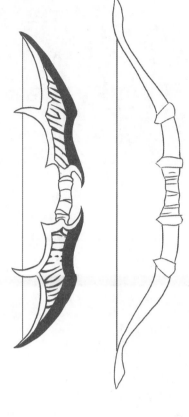

AXE

Often used by dwarves in fantasy stories, axes are top-heavy and straight, with a curved blade. They are usually designed to be held in two hands, although hand axes can fit neatly into a single hand. As with swords, axes come in a variety of styles. Here are two very different designs to give you some ideas.

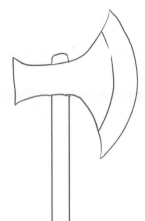

SPEARS AND POLEARMS

Spears and polearms are standard fantasy weapons. Spears have a sharp pointed metal tip at the end and polearms can have a variety of attachments or none at all. Their simple design can make them tricky to customise, but adding details along the pole is one way you could try to make your designs feel more unique.

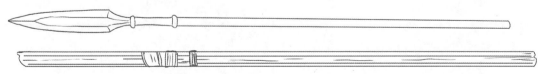

DEPICTING MAGICAL EFFECTS

Magical effects are often used in fantasy artwork. Flames, ice and sparkles usually come from a single point, such as a wand, finger or staff. The examples below will give you some ideas, but once you've mastered these you can experiment with other forms.

Start with a rough sketch to get the shape and size of the effect you want. Once you have this in place, you can add in more detail, depending on the type of magical effect you want to portray. Below are some examples of magical effects that you can try!

SPARKLES

One of the simplest effects to draw, sparkles are simply a smattering of stars and orbs. Add small cloud-like shapes to give the misty effect of sparkles. These are useful effects for a magical storyline.

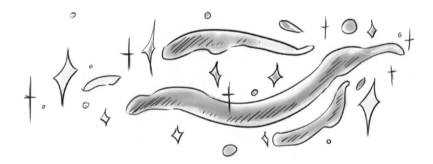

FLAMES

Flames are hard to capture, but there are some simple tricks you can use. Think of the edge of a sawtooth blade – use this as the basic shape, and then build it up to create a varied and interesting flame effect. Draw smaller flames around the edge to give the fire a more realistic appearance.

ICE

Ice is angular and jagged, so be sure to incorporate a lot of sharp points along the shape.

BLASTS

Think explosion! Blasts are energetic forces that usually emanate from ball shapes. Keep the shapes curved and add circular shapes coming out along the length of the blast to show this energetic effect.

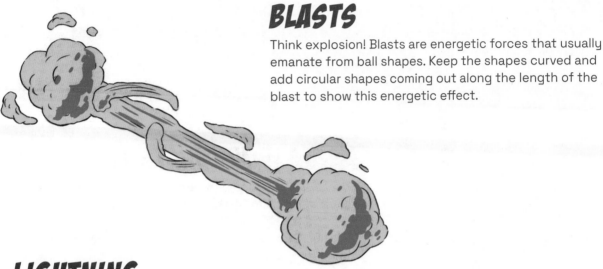

LIGHTNING

A crackled effect with branching angled lines – take your basic sketch and draw arched forks along it, then thicken these to give the effect of lightning.

MAGIC WAND

Any of these effects can come from a single point such as a magic wand. Here you can see a simple wand shape and the direction in which the effects shoot out.

WINGS AND HORNS

Wings and horns are often part of drawing fantasy creatures, and so learning how to draw these features will help you create more varied and interesting characters. If you're starting out, it's a great idea to look at as many references as you can, including those found on real-life animals.

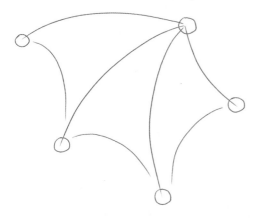

BASIC WING SHAPES

Animals like bats and birds are a great reference for the shape of wings for fantasy characters. The basic form of a wing is the same for both feathered and unfeathered varieties. Start with a small circle to represent the joint that connects the wing to the body. Then map out the other joints using curved connector lines.

UNFEATHERED WINGS

For unfeathered wings, understanding the structure of the wing is very important. Take the basic structure of the wing as explained above, then flesh it out, making sure to keep the bones visible beneath the membrane. Add weight to your lines to thicken out the wing. The spaces between the connectors form the wing itself. Draw curved lines between the wingtips to create the full wing, and add texture as you go to give the feel of skin.

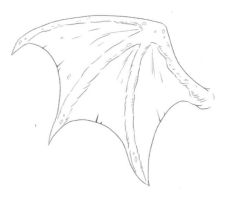

FEATHERED WINGS

To draw realistic feathered wings, it helps to understand the form of a feather. The shape of a feather starts with a slightly curved line, with fibres emanating from that centre line. There are many different kinds of feathers, but they often follow this shape. When constructing a feathered wing, you don't need to draw each individual feather but pay attention to the overall silhouette, as shown here.

HORNS

Like wings, horns are found in the natural world, so you will be able to source lots of reference images to help you draw them. Look at images of goats, rhinos or any other creature that has horns and this will give you a great starting point. Here are a few examples to give you some more ideas.

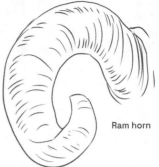

Ram horn

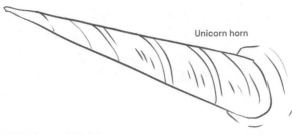

Unicorn horn

Short demon horn

Draw rough circles on the head of your character for the position of the base of each horn. Add rough outlines of the horns. Then you can add details like texture and shadows.

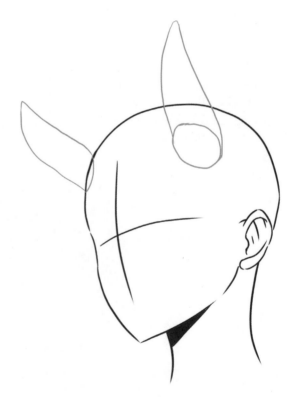

WORLD BUILDING

A fantasy world is full of intrigue, mystery and magic, so you will need to give the look of your settings the same level of detail as your characters and imagined creatures.

A SENSE OF PLACE

Creating a map of your world is one way to give yourself a reference point. It will help you maintain consistency and is an exciting way to add depth to your world. To get started, it's useful to draw on graph paper, as this can help you plot roads, houses and other elements that you would find on a typical map.

As with this example, you can start your world with a small town. From here you can expand outwards into a wider area to include mountain ranges, rivers, oceans and cities. You can experiment with town names and other landmarks to create a sense of place when looking at your world.

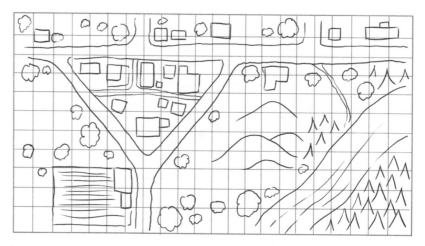

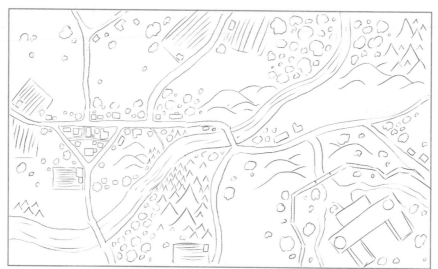

THE STYLE OF YOUR WORLD

Establishing a style for your setting is important too. Watching fantasy movies and reading fantasy books and comics can give you visual references for your own work. What sort of place are you inspired by? Here is an idea for a naturalistic world.

YOUR WORLD'S TIME PERIOD

What sort of timeframe do you want your world to be set in? A lot of fantasy manga takes place in a pseudo-medieval world, so looking at references of that time period will help you to imagine a place. But it doesn't have to be restricted to this – how about the Roman period? Or ancient Egyptian? Or was it a time before notable architecture that doesn't feature buildings at all? This scene is an idea for an ancient Japanese world.

DRAGONS

Dragons are one of the most striking fantasy creatures. Eastern dragons are wingless, serpent-like forces for good, while Western dragons tend to be dangerous creatures with wings and more bulky body shapes. On these pages you'll see how to draw a Western dragon.

1 Make a simple framework using basic shapes. Start with a rectangle to mimic the dragon's head, wider at the base and thinner at the nose. Use circles of varying sizes to simulate joints, like those of the wings. Use connecting lines to form the basis of the spine and tail.

2 Connect the edges of the basic shapes using simple lines. You will start to see the shape of the neck, tail and torso. Fill out the dragon wings with big, swooping lines from each wingtip.

3 Fill out the body curves, muscles and sharp angles. To complete the drawing, add more details, specifically textures. Add feathers, scales or horns to fully flesh it out.

4 The final stage is to add colour, which you may choose to do if your dragon is part of a colourful scene.

GOBLINS, TROLLS AND MONSTERS

Goblins, trolls and other monster shapes can be tricky to draw, as they have different proportions to the average human. However, you can use your understanding of the proportions of the human body and experiment to create something more monstrous and fantastical.

For these kinds of creatures, begin with a human wireframe and then play around with the proportions. Do this by replacing the circles with larger ones, representing larger joints and limbs. Widening the hips and stance can also help to create a more monstrous physique, with the head sitting lower than you would see on a standard human wireframe. Don't be afraid to experiment!

When filling out your wireframes, make sure to include details like the musculature of the limbs and body, as this helps create the shape of a monstrous being. Emphasising these details will help bring your creature to life. Here are some examples.

GOBLINS

Goblins are typically short, with a heavy lower body and thinner limbs. Their faces follow a human shape but with specific variations – the nose is often elongated and bulbous, with small eyes and pointed ears. Place emphasis on the pot belly to really enhance their unusual shape.

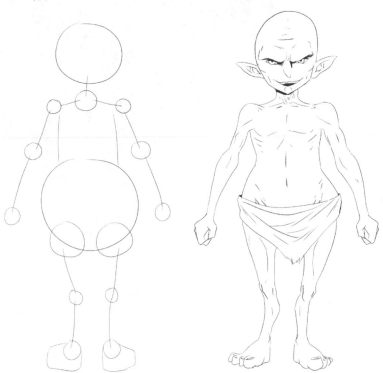

TROLLS

To draw a troll, take the shape of a goblin and add weight to it – a lot of weight! The proportions between the two creatures are very similar, although the troll's legs are longer. Ensuring that the joints are large and weighty should help you to get the feel of a troll. The same approach can also be used with other similar monsters, like cyclops.

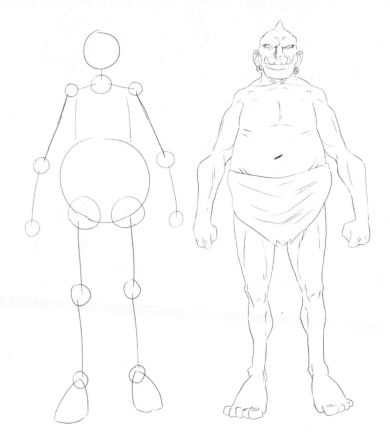

MONSTERS

Monsters come in many different forms, so you can really start to play around with different shapes and proportions. They may not have arms or legs, or they may have multiples of each. You might want to leave space in the torso of your wireframe for additional arms, appendages, or even tentacles!

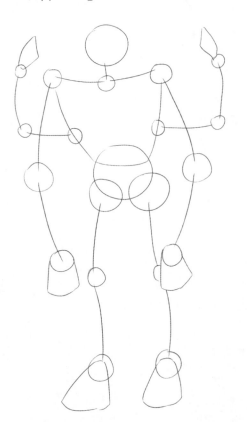

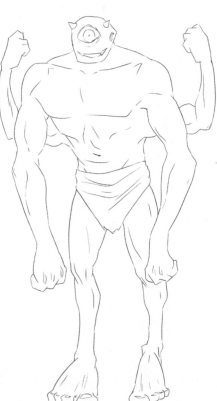

CENTAURS

Centaurs have the torso and head of a human and the body of a horse. To understand the shape of a centaur, you need to practise drawing horses, as this will make the base of your creature. You have already seen how to draw the human body (see page 18), so now it's time to focus on the horse body.

1 Start with the horse's body. Draw two circles connected by sloping lines. In most horses, the top line slopes gently down toward the ground with the curve of the spine. The bottom line curves away from the ground, filling out the rib cage and belly. Draw the legs, using two circles connected by sloping lines for each one, and add inverted teacup shapes as the hooves. You can move the circles as needed to bend or reposition the legs.

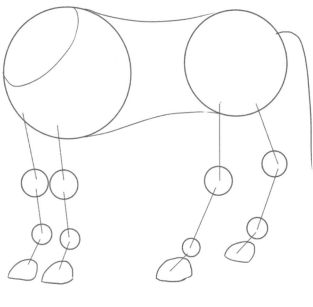

2 Once you have your basic sketch, it's time to fill in the details. Centaur bodies are as muscular as horses bodies, so be sure to show this when defining the body shape.

3 The human portion of the centaur fits where the neck and head of the horse would be. Sketch it out as you would for a male body, making sure the connection between the horse body and the hips is aligned, then draw the human shape as required.

4 Fill out your wireframe body to match the muscular form of the horse body. It's easy to mismatch these halves, so make sure that your finished drawing looks like one creature.

DWARVES AND HALFLINGS

As with goblins and trolls, dwarves and halflings are shorter in stature and stouter than humans, so to draw them you'll start with wider wireframes. However, they have more human features than goblins or trolls.

DWARVES

1 Dwarves are stocky and muscular, so factor this in when sketching out the wireframe. As you bulk out their form, make sure to pay extra attention to the width.

2 Add the details of the body. This is one example of a typical dwarf.

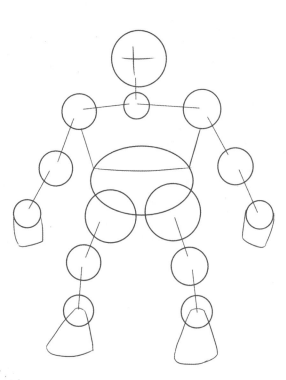

BEARDS

Dwarves are known for their incredible beards! Let's take a look at drawing their luscious facial locks.

1 Draw the face shape with an outline of hair around the mouth and up to the ears. Add the beard by drawing hair flowing down from the chin.

2 Once you have the basic shape of the beard, pick out strands of the hair, and add texture. You can add plaits, beads and jewellery to the beard to give it extra character and detail.

HALFLINGS

Short in stature like dwarves but not as muscular, halflings are known for their chubby faces, smaller pointed ears and large feet. When drawing your wireframe, make sure you emphasise the larger feet – and don't forget the hairy toes! Here you can see how the wireframe should be shaped to complete your drawing.

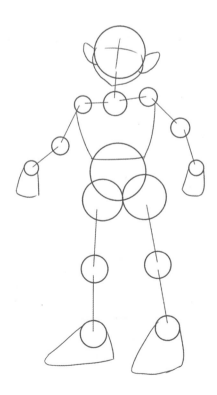

ELVES

Elves are common fantasy characters that you might want to add to your drawings. The most obvious differences between elves and other human-like characters are their graceful form and pointed ears. They also often have very long, defined hair and lithe bodies and faces. As their ears are their most prominent features, let's start here.

EARS

Take the outline of a human ear and extend the shape upwards at the tip. There can be many variations on elves' ears: they can be made longer or shorter than average, set close to the head or sticking out.

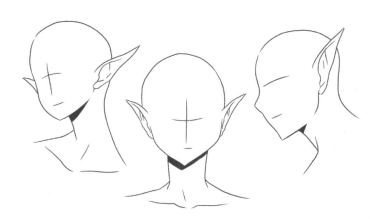

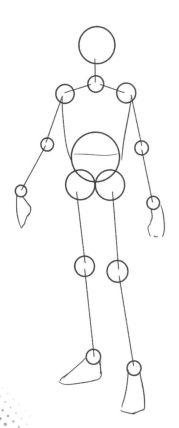

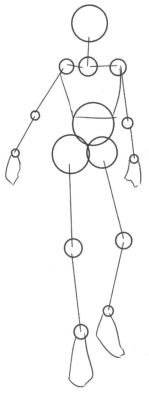

BODY SHAPES

Elves are known for their lithe forms. When constructing a wireframe for an elf, keep their hips and shoulders slim, and when filling out the face, make it thinner and more angular than a human face. The hair is typically long, straight and flowing.

ELF CLOTHING

Elven fashion is very nature-orientated, with delicate spirals and natural forms like leaves. For this, looking at references in nature, like oak leaves, will help. These features can also be present in their armour and weapons.

Elven clothing is often flowing in design, with lots of emphasis on robes and draping fabrics.

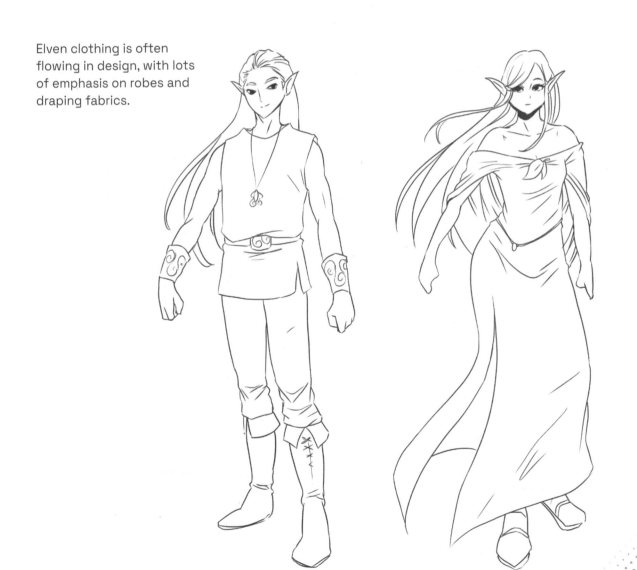

WEREWOLVES

Werewolves are huge creatures that loom over the landscape, so drawing them on a large scale is important. They are similar in shape to wolves, so we'll begin by drawing a wolf's head before moving on to the rest of the body.

1 Begin by drawing an oval, rather than a circle. Then draw a centre line down the oval to help you plot the facial features of the wolf.

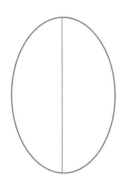

2 Next, draw a line across the oval 1/3 of the way down from the top of the head. This is the eyeline. Draw another line 2/3 down the oval for the mouth. Then sketch a rough trapezoid shape between these two lines to represent the snout, and add the ears.

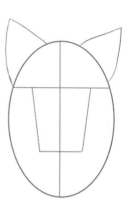

3 Add in the eyes – they should be small and sit snugly at the top of the trapezoid shape. Draw a curved line along the bottom line for the mouth and add the nose above this.

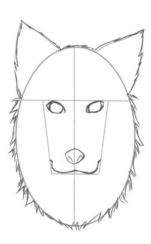

4 To complete the face, flesh out the fur around the head shape, keeping the strokes light and flicking outwards. Add in texture and details to give the wolf's head depth.

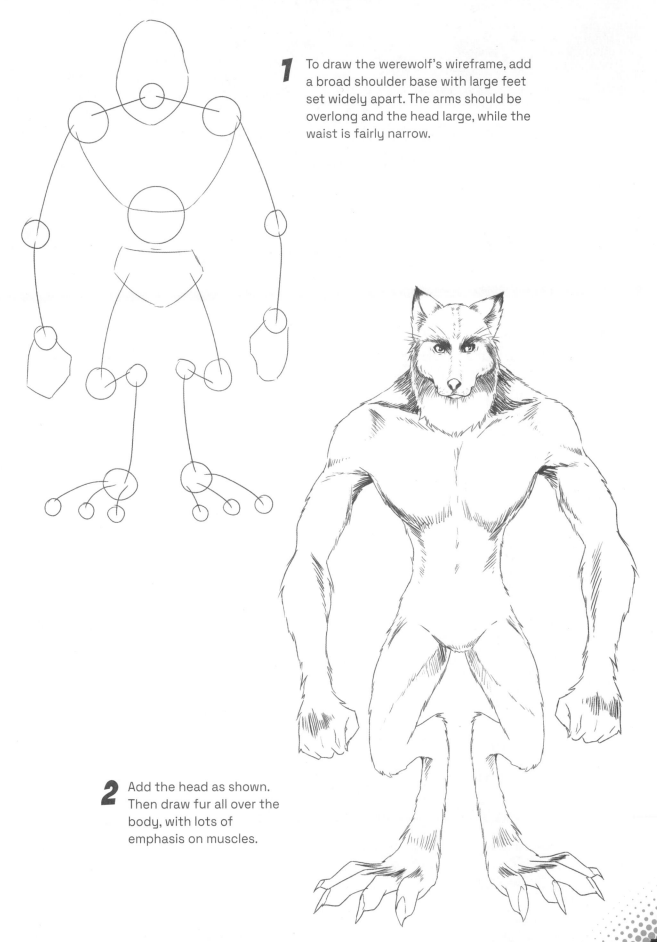

1 To draw the werewolf's wireframe, add a broad shoulder base with large feet set widely apart. The arms should be overlong and the head large, while the waist is fairly narrow.

2 Add the head as shown. Then draw fur all over the body, with lots of emphasis on muscles.

FAIRIES

Fairies are magical creatures that are known for their fun and mischievous nature. When drawing them, pay attention to their body language and facial expressions as well as giving them their most well-known feature: their wings!

FAIRY WINGS

Fairy wings are different to the structured wings on page 38 – they don't have joints in the same way. Butterflies, dragonflies, bees and wasps are all great reference material for fairy wings.

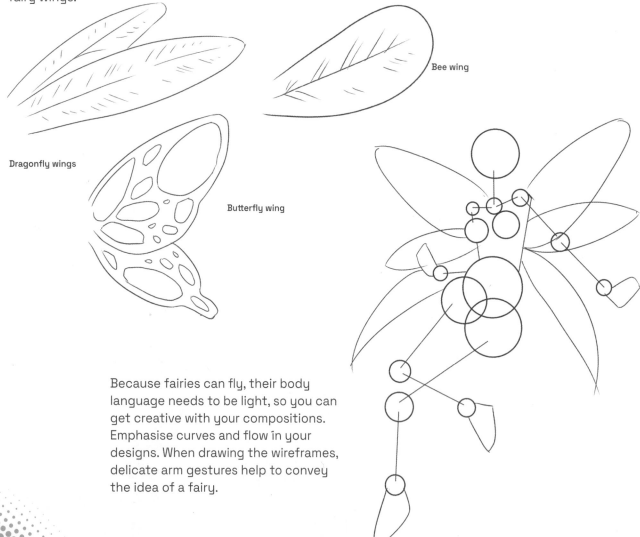

Dragonfly wings

Bee wing

Butterfly wing

Because fairies can fly, their body language needs to be light, so you can get creative with your compositions. Emphasise curves and flow in your designs. When drawing the wireframes, delicate arm gestures help to convey the idea of a fairy.

FAIRY FASHION

Fairy fashion, like elven fashion, is very nature-based, so using references of leaves and flowers can help greatly with your fairy character. They also frequently have pointed ears like those of elves, so including these will help you create a believable fairy.

EXAMPLE CHARACTERS

Here are some ideas of fantasy characters that you can create for your manga world. Once you've mastered the basic skills needed to draw the human form, you can adapt them to draw any creature you can imagine.

CHIBI

CHIBI

Chibi is a style of manga character that is very small with an oversized head and very little detail. Chibi is also known as SD or Super Deformation, as what defines this style is the chubby, squashed proportions and exaggerated, simplified expressions of the characters. Let's get cute!

CHIBI PROPORTIONS

Chibi style can be broken down into different proportions. These are 1:2, 1:3 and 1:4, with the numbers representing the relationship between the size of the head and the height of the whole figure. It is a good idea to use these measurements to map out your character, rather than trying to guess what proportions will work.

1 When the body is the same size as the head the proportion is 1:2 (because the figure is two heads high). This creates the smallest, cutest, most exaggerated body shape commonly associated with chibi style. With these proportions you are restricted with the details you can add due to the smaller size of the character.

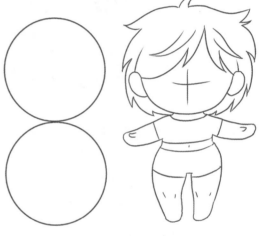

2 The next size used, 1:3, adds an additional head of space, so the chibi is three heads high. This allows for more detail in your character. This is the most common chibi proportion and a good place to start if you're new to drawing this style of character.

3 The proportion 1:4 adds a further head of space and is closer to the standard proportions you see in manga. It is much more like the regular proportions of a child.

PROPORTIONS OF THE CHIBI FACE

Along with the body, the chibi face changes according to the proportions used. The most obvious difference is in the size of the eyes, which are much larger than those of regular manga characters, allowing chibis to have a greater range of expression.

1 If you're drawing using the 1:2 proportions for the body, the facial features are the most exaggerated, with the eyes becoming the most dominant feature in terms of size. The ears also become larger.

2 With the proportions 1:3, the facial features of the character are less distorted than when you use the 1:2 proportions. The eyes, ears and mouth are slightly smaller in proportion to the rest of the face.

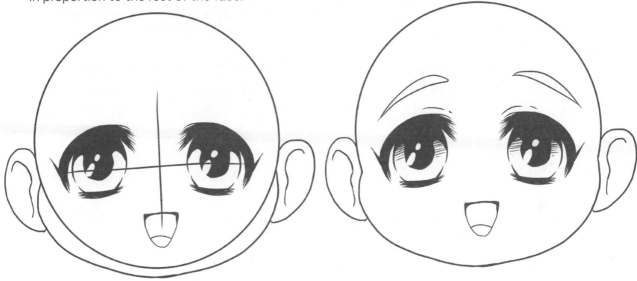

3 The features when using the 1:4 proportions are similar to those of a child and can be used both for chibi and regular manga characters.

SHRINKING THE HANDS AND FEET

When drawing chibi characters, you need to reduce the size of the finer details like the hands and feet. Keep in mind the head ratio you are using and modify as needed.

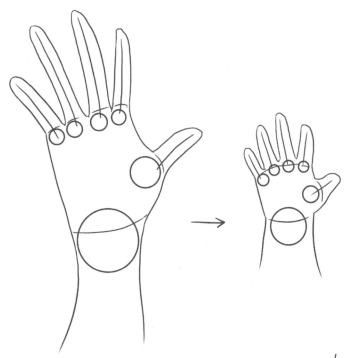

When using smaller proportions like 1:2, you don't need to include all the fingers and can just draw a small thumb. With the other proportions, the hands become chubbier and rounder, with the fingers having minimal detail and movement. Think of it as taking off the last joint of the fingers and expressing any gestures with less detail.

Apply the same principles when drawing the feet. Use the basic method of drawing feet as shown on page 15, but take the larger triangle and circle and shrink them down to a chubbier, cuter version.

THUMBNAIL POSES

As chibi manga has distorted shapes, it can be difficult to plot your composition using the wireframe approach. Thumbnailing is a useful process where you create a very small, simple sketch in a short timeframe. This helps you to brainstorm composition ideas, and works well with chibi's art style.

When creating thumbnails, plotting the overall composition should take precedent over the individual components that make up a wireframe. Use head ratios to help plot this and, when sketching, ensure you preserve the roundness of the character, as this is typical of the style.

These thumbnails should take you no longer than 10 minutes each. As you practise, this process will become faster and easier, allowing you to come up with more ideas in a short space of time. Once you're happy with your chibi, pick your favourite composition and work on it further.

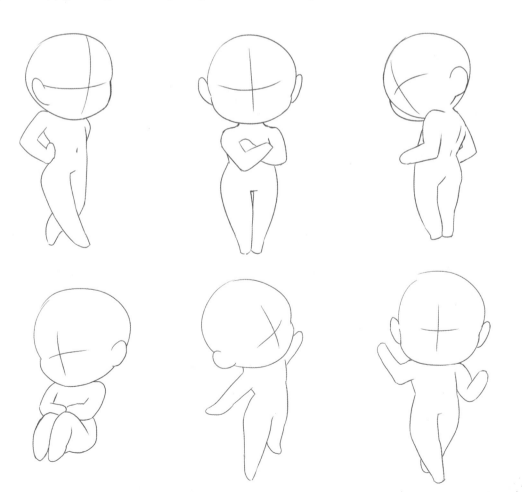

FROM SKETCH TO FINISHED CHIBI

To go from thumbnail to sketch, enlarge the overall shape and add some definition to your character. This is when you can draw elements that will bring your character to life – the hair and the expressions. Make sure that your chibi looks like a super-exaggerated version of the character you thumbnailed.

Remember, the hair and eyes are always enlarged in this step, so don't be afraid to get creative with this and over-exaggerate these elements. Once you're happy, it's time to move on to the next step: extra details.

ADDING CHIBI DETAILS

Now you can dress your chibi character! For an authentic chibi look, keep the style simple and child-like.

Sketch the clothes over the top of the chibi body shape, including the key details. When sketching the clothing, you don't need to put as many crease lines and details around the body parts as you would for a full-size character, so don't be afraid to keep things simple.

The same goes for details like jewellery and other accessories – simplify the shapes and don't add too many details. This cute character has a simple bow for her hair and some heart-shaped earrings.

LINEARTING AN IMAGE

The next step is to add the outline to your character – a process known as linearting. Lineart is permanent, so you must finalise your sketch before this step. Plan where you will draw before you commit pen to paper. You can correct your mistakes with white fluid should you need to, but this will affect the texture of the paper, so should be avoided.

1 Start from one side and move across the image, going over the pencil lines with ink. You shouldn't start the lineart in one corner of your image or jump around the drawing as your hand could accidentally smudge the lines as the ink is drying.

2 Once you have completed the basic lineart, go back over the areas where there is shadow and where the lines meet each other. Thicken these areas up to give a sense of depth to your drawing. This will help the colouring to really stand out (see pages 68–69). Add further detail and shadows in stages. Wait for these areas to dry and then use an eraser to remove the pencil lines.

ADDING COLOUR

Once your lineart is complete, it's time to add some colour! This can be done using marker pens, or you can convert the drawing into a digital version and use a computer program to add the colour. Drawing directly onto a tablet or computer to start with will save you a step.

The principles of adding tone and colour are the same whether you're using pens or a computer. It's up to you which method you prefer to use.

COLOURING WITH MARKERS

If you are working using pen and paper alone, you can come up with some amazing colour finishes using marker pens.

1 Once you have your completed lineart image as described on pages 66–67, the next stage is to add colour. Start with the flat colours – you'll add the shading later.

2 Plot the source of light and decide where the darker shadows will be.

3 Add shading in lighter and darker colours or tones to complete your work.

COLOURING DIGITALLY

To make your drawing into a digital image, photograph it with a high-resolution camera and turn up the contrast to ensure any remaining pencil marks are masked. Alternatively, you can scan the image onto a computer using a flatbed scanner. Once you have digitised the image, it's time to start colouring.

1 Import your image into the program of your choice. If your linearted image has been merged with a white background, you will need to change the layer style to 'multiply' to be able to see the colouring underneath. Create a new layer and colour in as you would with markers, adding flat colours. Plot where the light source will be in your image.

2 With the light source established, you can decide where to place the shadows on the body. Colour in these areas with a dark navy blue. When working digitally, navy is preferable to black; when you turn down the opacity of this layer on your computer program, navy creates a more colourful effect, while black washes out the colour underneath. Once you're done, turn the opacity of this layer down to 60%.

3 The final step is to add some white highlights in the places where the light hits. In this example, it's the top of the head and the cheeks. Now you have a finished chibi character!

CHIBI ANIMALS

It's not just humans that can get the chibi treatment – animals are often 'chibi-fied' to create a whole range of fun characters. Using the same process as on pages 58-59, you can turn any animal into a chibi.

1 Start by choosing a simple animal shape, such as a rabbit. Find some references before you start to get an idea of how your animal looks. Using the 1:2 proportions on page 58, plot the outline of the animal, simplifying the shape as you go.

2 Pick out the most recognisable elements of your animal and make these prominent. With a rabbit, for example, you might pick the ears, the feet and the face. This style is about conveying the idea of the rabbit rather than a realistic depiction. Try drawing your animal in different, fun poses.

MORE CHIBI ANIMALS

Once you have got the concept of drawing one chibi animal, you can apply it to all sorts of different creatures!

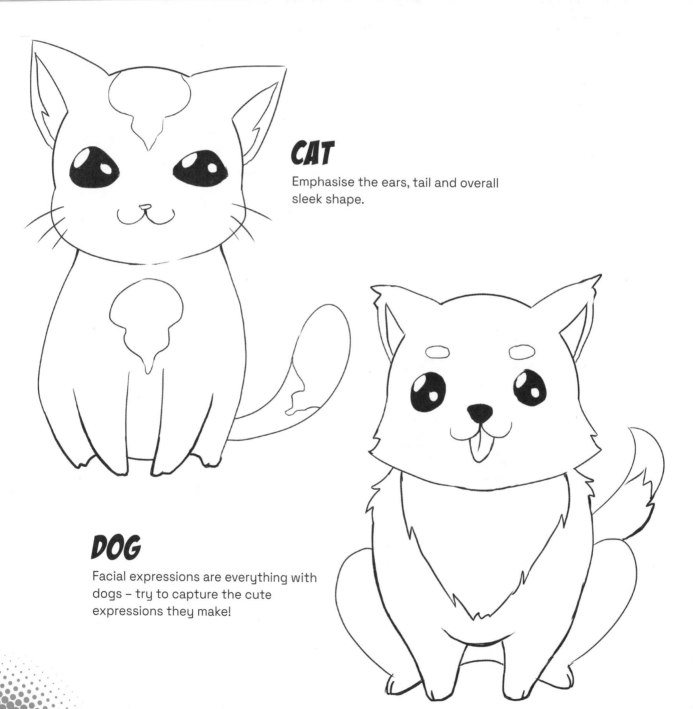

CAT

Emphasise the ears, tail and overall sleek shape.

DOG

Facial expressions are everything with dogs – try to capture the cute expressions they make!

TIGER

Like a cat, but with stripes!

LION

You can't go wrong with a big, cute mane!

CHIBI MASCOTS

A common feature in manga, mascots combine elements of human chibis with animal features. Their usual purpose is to provide comedic effect, so make yours as cute and as funny as possible. The example below is just one option, but the possibilities are endless!

1 Take the head of a rabbit and add a simple chibi body.

2 Then add some exciting features. What about a long tail and some wings? There is no end to how creative you can get when brainstorming a new mascot!

3 For a really cute chibi mascot, use pretty pastel shades to colour it in.

MECHA

MECHA

Let's delve into the sci-fi genre with mecha manga!
Mecha is short for mechanised armour and is a
common staple in many manga comics. Famous titles
in this style include *Gundam* and *Evangelion*, and
they're worth checking out.

MECHA ARMOUR

Most mecha characters have armour in order to protect themselves in battle. You can start off by taking the elements of traditional of fantasy armour (pages 32–33) and altering them. Here you can see a fantasy suit of armour next to mecha armour. All the components are the same but the shapes for the mecha are more angular.

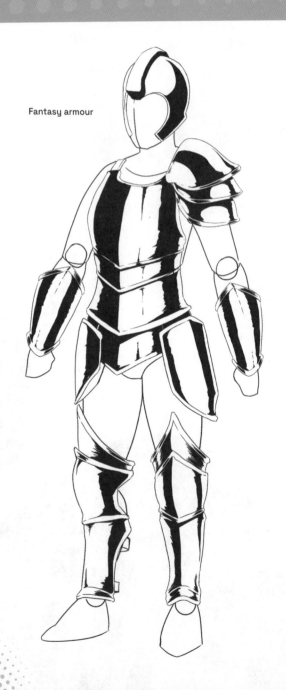

Fantasy armour

Mecha armour

MECHA HELMET STYLES

There are different types of mecha characters, each with their own style. Here we will look at Gundam-style, Evangelion-style and bodysuit-style mecha helmets.

GUNDAM

Gundam mecha features enormous robots controlled by human pilots. They are the largest mecha and are made up of many blocky elements.

Gundam helmet

Evangelion helmet

EVANGELION

These mecha are more human in appearance and are typically smaller than Gundam. There are fewer straight lines in these designs, as they emulate the human form.

BODYSUIT

The smallest mecha wear close-fitting outfits over a human body, so you'll begin by drawing human proportions and adding a suit around that form.

Bodysuit helmet

MECHA DETAILS

When drawing mecha, it's the details that will make it unique. A robot is an engineered piece of machinery, so you need to understand a little about how it works. This will give you a better idea about how to illustrate the character when it is in motion.

Think about how the legs and arms connect to the body and what these joints should look like. For example, are they ball joints, and can you see the joints and seams?

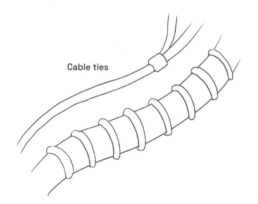

Cable ties

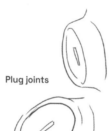

Plug joints

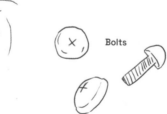

Ball joint

Bolts

Creating a silhouette of your mecha can help you come up with a unique design that will stand out from the many others already out there. Try drawing an outline without extra details.

Additional details you might add include wires, nuts, bolts, units, buttons or computers. These will be style-specific – the bulkier the mecha, the more likely you are to see elements like nuts and bolts; the sleeker the mecha, the more units and wires you will see.

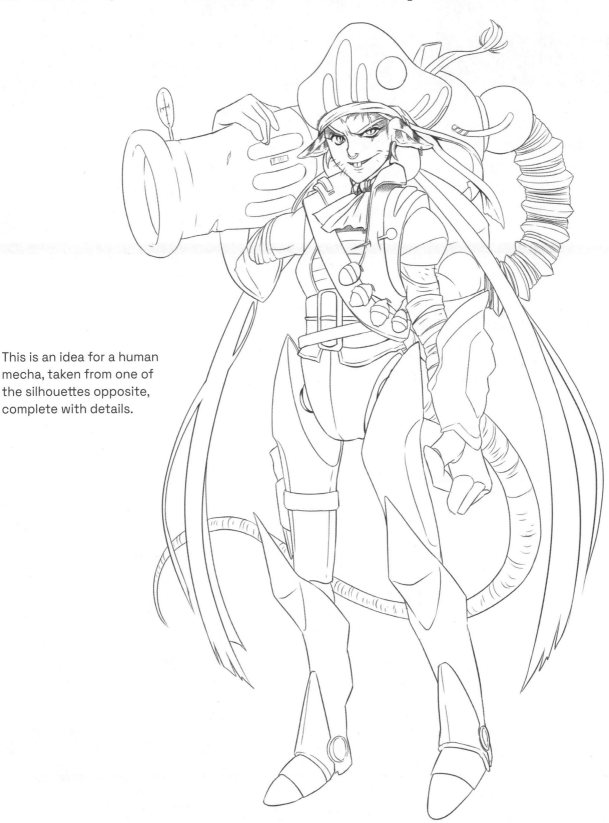

This is an idea for a human mecha, taken from one of the silhouettes opposite, complete with details.

GUNDAM-STYLE MECHA: HEAD

Gundam heads are similar to human heads, but on a larger scale. They usually have two eyes and space for features resembling a mouth. The ears may look like human ears or you might have wings or other fantasy details instead.

1 When sketching the head, start with a cube-like shape rather than a circle. This immediately gives a mecha-like feel to your character. Draw a square shape with rounded corners inside the cube.

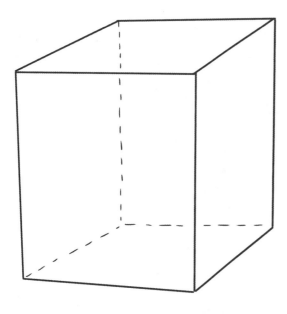

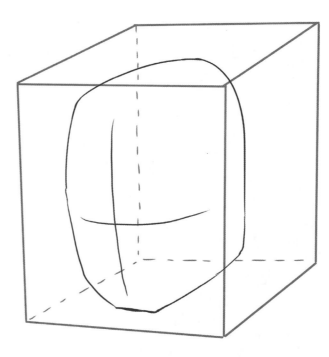

2 Experiment with different angles to see how it will look in various positions.

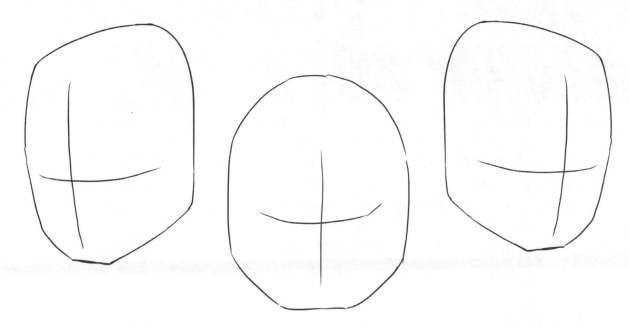

3 Once you're happy with the shape, add details using armour and machinery as your inspiration. Remember that the mecha exists in 3D space – there should be depth to the details of the helmet, as shown here. Make sure you can see the edges of these parts.

GUNDAM-STYLE MECHA: BODY

To draw a Gundam-style mecha body, you will use a number of cube shapes. Refer back to 2- and 3-point perspectives on pages 26–27 to draw 3D cubes so your mecha looks right.

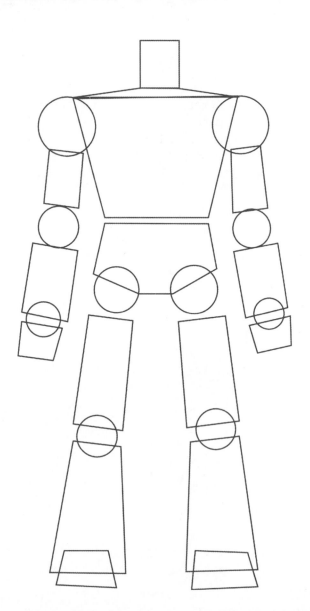

1 Start by drawing a wireframe mecha. The shapes used in a standard wireframe are applicable here – circles represent the joints and lines represent the limbs. However, the scale for Gundam-style is much larger than a standard human figure.

2 Once you have a wireframe to give you an idea of the overall design, start to apply cube shapes onto the limbs and body. Make sure you leave plenty of space for the chest, as this is the most likely place for your pilot's cockpit.

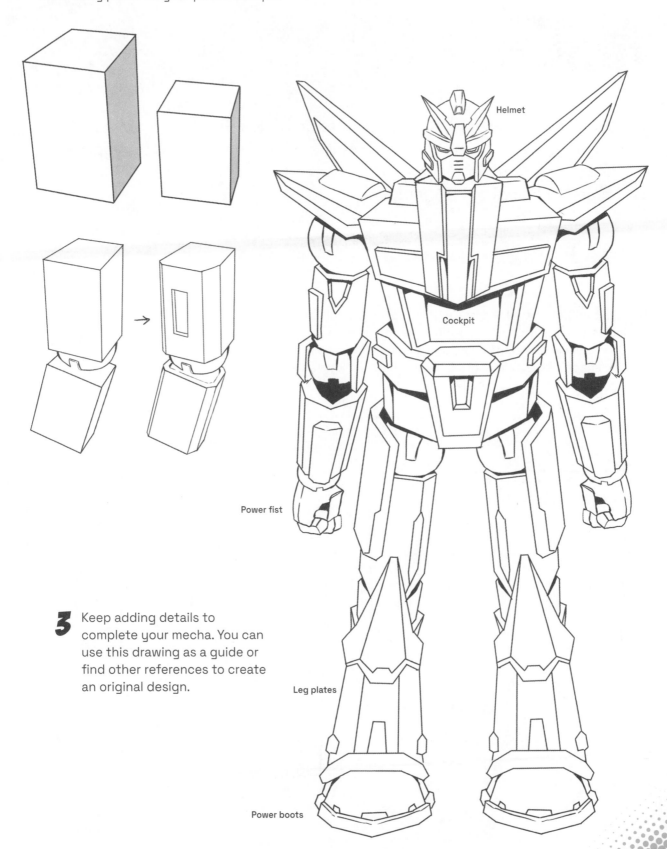

Helmet

Cockpit

Power fist

3 Keep adding details to complete your mecha. You can use this drawing as a guide or find other references to create an original design.

Leg plates

Power boots

EVANGELION-STYLE MECHA: HEAD

When drawing Evangelion-style mecha heads, think of them as halfway between humans and robots. You can use more curved lines than you did for the Gundam mecha, but they are still oversized mechanical beings that are piloted by humans.

1 Like the Gundam helmet, begin your Evangelion helmet drawing inside a cube – this will instantly make the shape more robotic. Draw a circle inside the cube, then begin to add a helmet shape. The shape of the helmet gives the mecha its unique style, so don't be afraid to get creative.

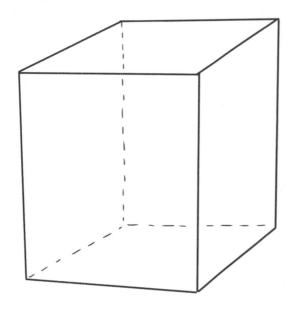

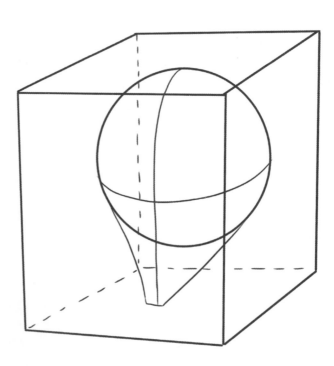

2 Try drawing the head shape from different angles so you know how it looks in various positions.

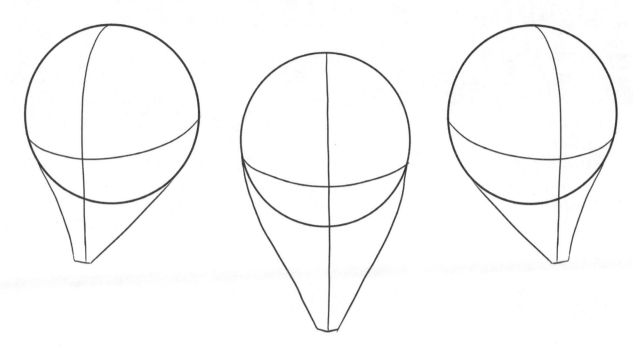

3 Add details in a similar style to the Gundam head – mechanical shapes, ear wings and bolts are all great additions.

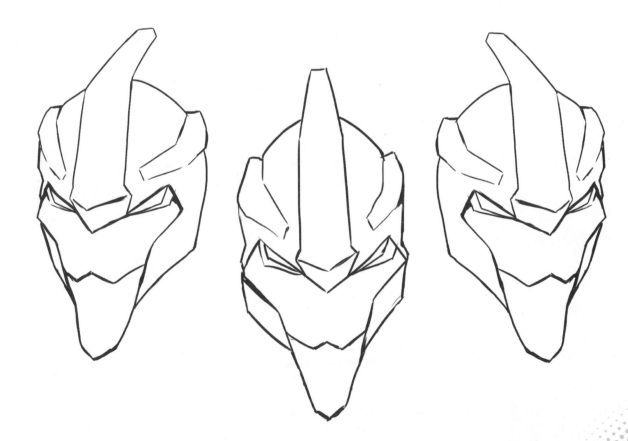

EVANGELION-STYLE MECHA: BODY

As with the head, the Evangelion-style body incorporates elements of the human body into its design, so its overall composition can look slightly humanoid. This means that the wireframe of the Evangelion-style mecha can resemble that of a monster with exaggerated proportions, as on page 45.

1 Evangelion pilots sit in a cockpit, in the same way as Gundam pilots. Start the mecha by drawing a wireframe. Make the size of the chest and shoulders extra large to get the proportions right.

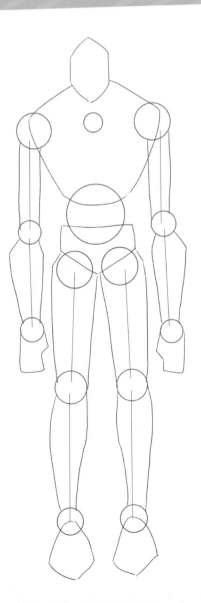

2 Flesh out the wireframe, remembering that you don't have to stick to straight lines here, and can incorporate more curved, human-like limbs.

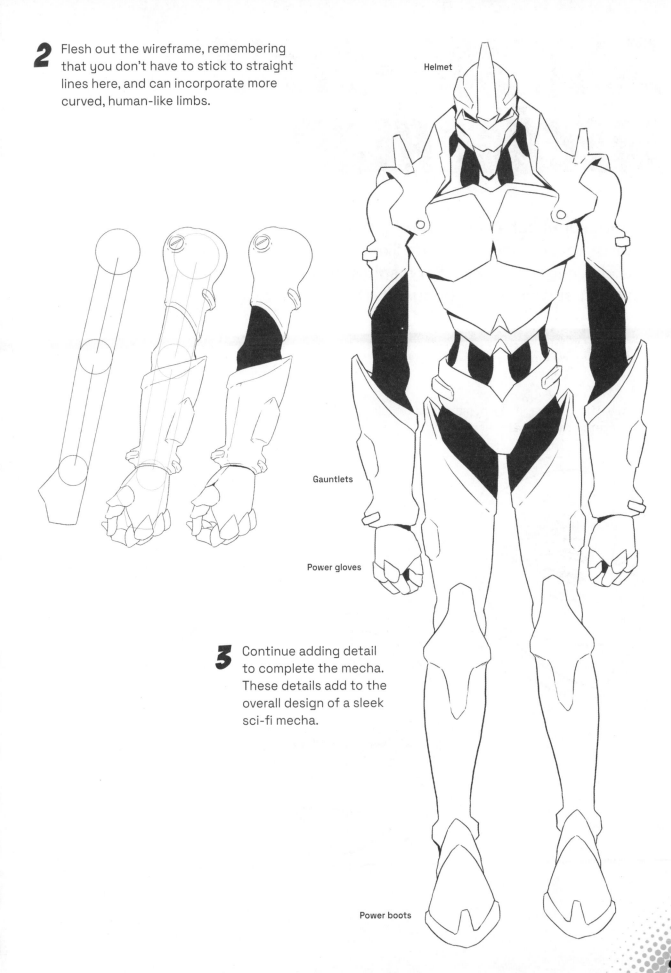

Helmet

Gauntlets

Power gloves

3 Continue adding detail to complete the mecha. These details add to the overall design of a sleek sci-fi mecha.

Power boots

BODYSUIT-STYLE MECHA: HEAD

Bodysuit mecha covers the form of the human body, so the shape of the head should be more like that of a helmet than the Gundam and Evangelion heads. For inspiration, check out images of Guyver, the most well-known bodysuit-style mecha.

1 Begin with the shape of a human head to help you sketch the helmet over it.

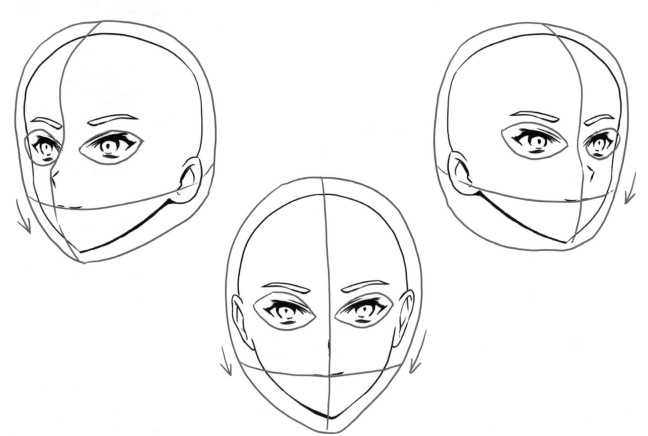

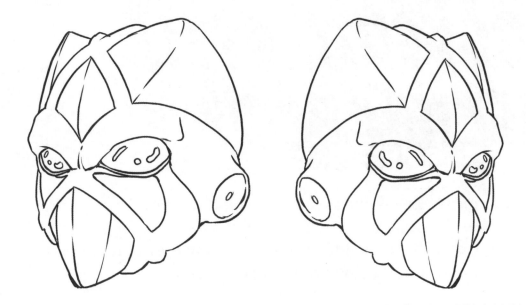

2 Next, flesh out possible designs, making the helmet as sleek as possible, with minimal details. Try drawing the head from different angles so that you can keep a consistent style when drawing the mecha in a story.

BODYSUIT-STYLE MECHA: BODY

A bodysuit-style mecha is drawn around a natural human frame, much like the standard body proportions shown on pages 18-19. These pages show one idea for a body suit that you can use for inspiration when drawing your own designs.

1 Begin by drawing a wireframe. This can be similar to human proportions, although you can elongate the arms and legs slightly if you wish. Add the outline of the mecha and erase the wireframe.

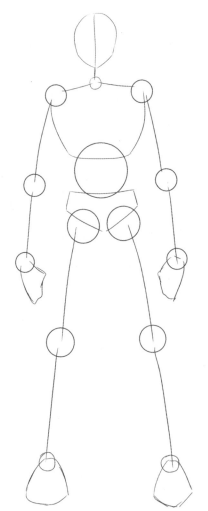

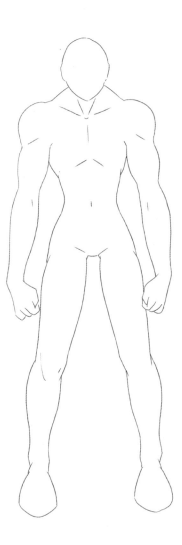

2 Add the details. The suit should fit snugly over the pilot. Consider how the suit is powered, whether it will need vents, as well as whether it needs the ability to travel in space. Thinking about all these elements will help you to flesh out your bodysuit mecha. You can also use elements of traditional armour (see pages 32–33) when creating your bodysuit mecha.

3 Keep adding details to complete your mecha. You can use this drawing as a guide or find other references to create an original design.

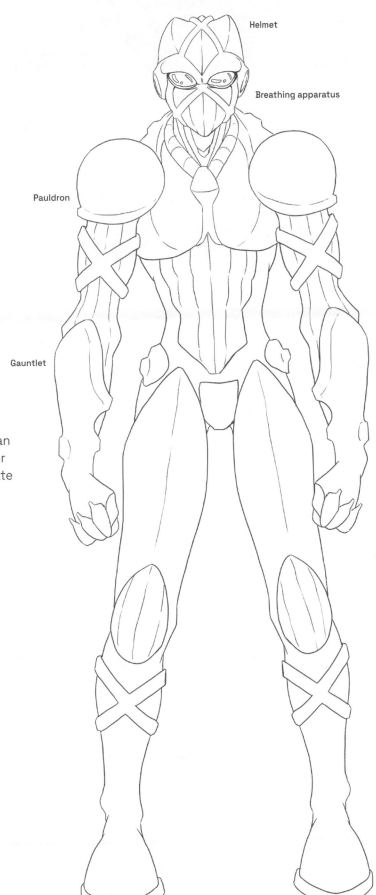

Helmet

Breathing apparatus

Pauldron

Gauntlet

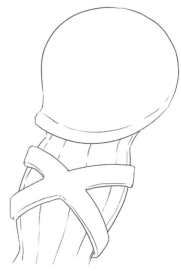

MECHA PILOT DESIGN

Mecha pilots are humans who are trained to drive mechas. They usually wear sleek bodysuits that fit snugly, allowing them to work and fight effectively. Take a look at manga reference if you're stuck for ideas, and use it to create your own pilot bodysuits.

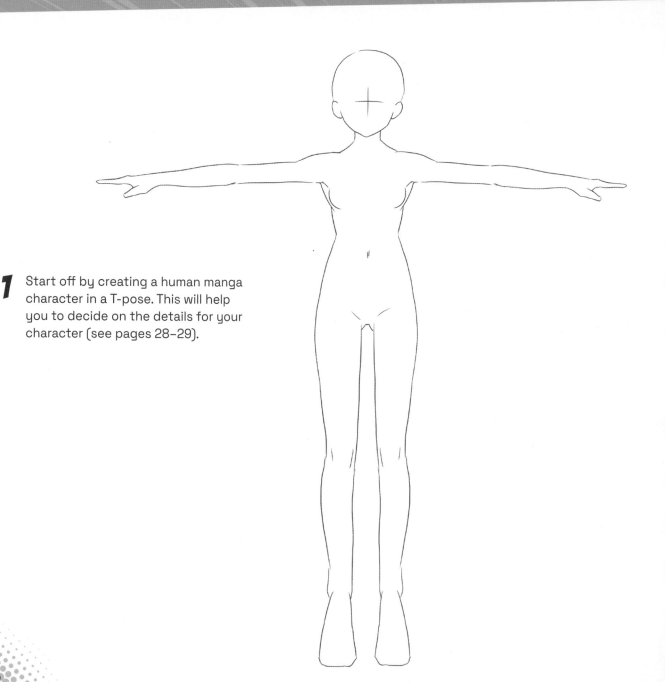

1 Start off by creating a human manga character in a T-pose. This will help you to decide on the details for your character (see pages 28–29).

2 Now add a blank bodysuit. Draw an outline around the body shape and then add some detail to the design of the bodysuit. You can add a motif to your bodysuit to make your character immediately identifiable.

Diamond motif

3 Consider extra details, like a breathing tube or waterproof shoes, and the way that these join to the suit. You can practise drawing them separately before adding them to your character. Some ideas are shown below.

Buttons

Ports

Plugs

Tubes

4 Your pilot may also need a helmet to go with the bodysuit. Think about the details when you are designing. Does the pilot need to breathe underwater? Are they travelling in space? Remember, mecha designs should be functional above all else.

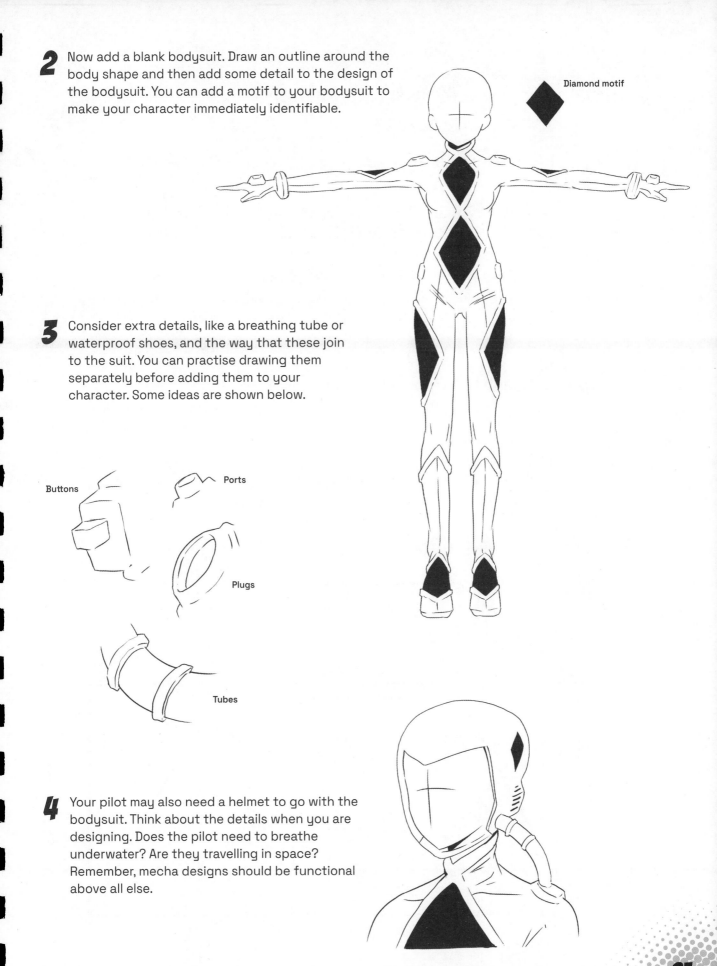

MECHA COCKPITS

Unless controlled by remote, most giant mecha have a cockpit that is the pilot's control room. Keep this in mind when designing your mecha, as it is a key part of its engineering. Think about how the pilot gets into the cockpit, and how they will fit into the cockpit and use its space. Are they seated? Are they standing? Do they need to be buckled in? Once you have made these decisions, it will become much easier for you to sketch it out. Writing a list of the cockpit's features can help with this process.

1 Start off by drawing a cube shape using a 1-point perspective. This will enable you to draw sight lines to make the angles more consistent.

2 Use the sight lines of this perspective to shape the cockpit and start to add key elements to the interior design, including the seat, screens and entrances. Add the remaining details – the more complete the design at this stage, the easier it will be to keep it consistent later on. Think of this as a map.

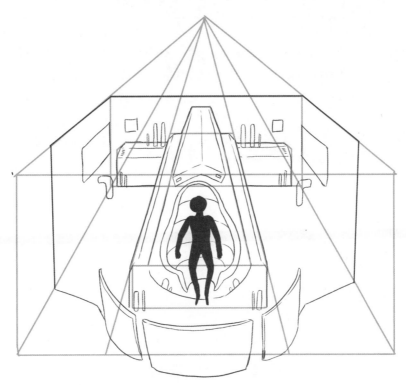

3 Once you are happy with your sketch, lineart the cockpit (see pages 66–67), erase your pencil lines and admire your engineering!

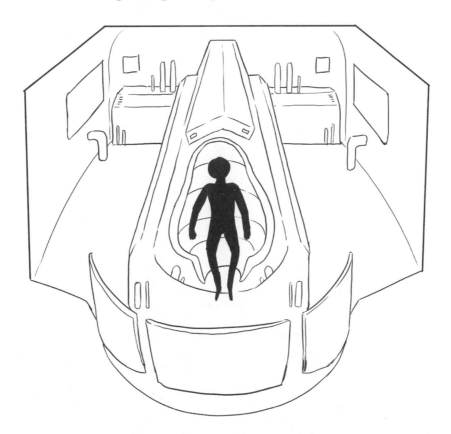

MECHA IN MOTION

It's time to make your mecha move – they're not just for display! You can use your wireframe to help visualise the movement of your mecha. Let's start with the basic wireframe of your design so far.

1 Start with the wireframe and try to visualise how it fits in 3D space. Think about what movements you want your mecha to make and whether or not it can make those movements based on its design. If your mecha has large shoulder pads, for example, it will not be able to lift its arms straight upwards, so take care to consider the logistics of your designs.

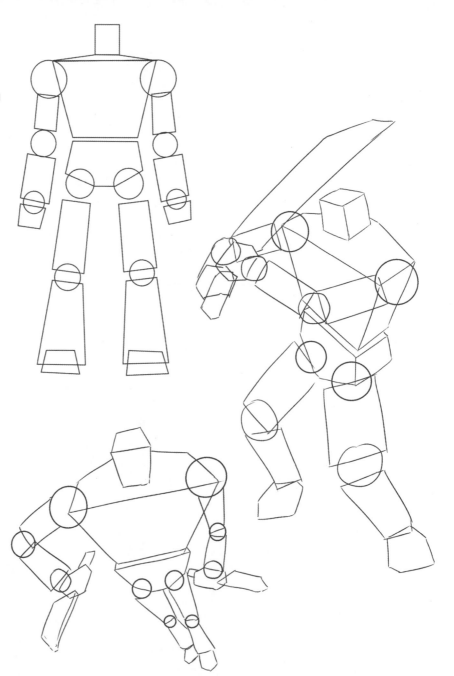

2 When you're happy with the composition of your mecha, start to fill out the wireframe, adding detail. If it helps, keep a two-point perspective horizon line in the background and use these lines to help bring your mecha to life.

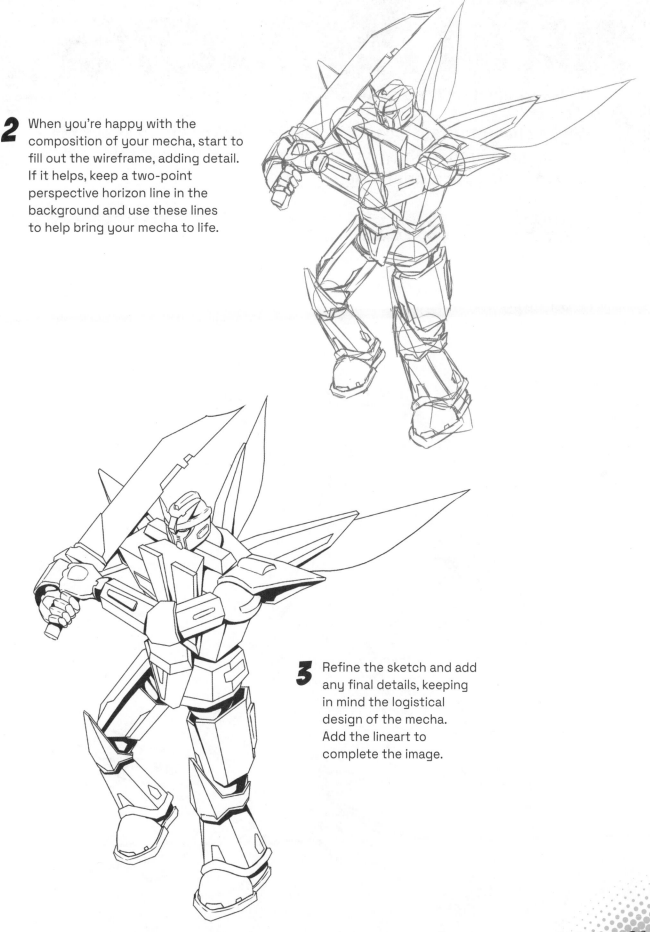

3 Refine the sketch and add any final details, keeping in mind the logistical design of the mecha. Add the lineart to complete the image.

MECHA DESTRUCTION

Mecha characters are big and heavy, so they're sure to affect the environment around them as they move about. Showing this will help to bring your story to life!

Mecha are extremely heavy pieces of machinery and one of the simplest ways to illustrate this weight is by manipulating the environment around them. Picture a heavy ball hitting the floor – it could leave a dent or even crack the surface. The same is true with mecha.

The heavy footsteps of this mecha have caused the ground to shatter!

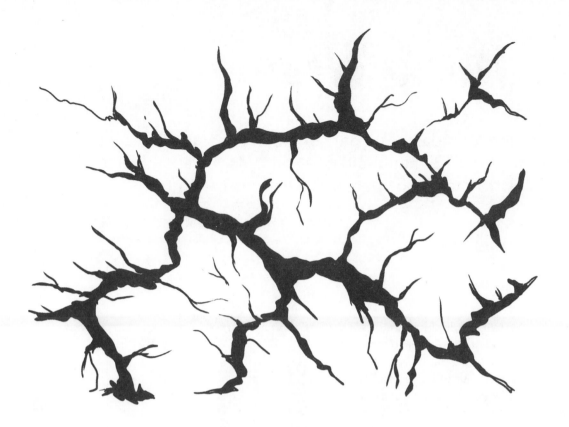

If you need inspiration for the destruction after a mecha has walked on the ground, look at images of dry riverbeds. The cracked effect is similar to that made by heavy objects on tarmac or concrete.

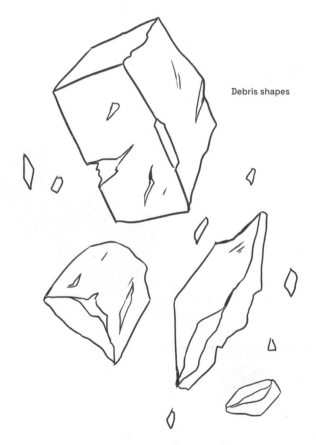

Debris shapes

Drawing boulders and smaller pieces of debris around your mecha will also give the idea that a robot has crashed through the area.

MECHA GUNS

Weapons are a fundamental part of mecha design. These weapons can be guns or other handheld weapons. Mecha are usually designed with their own specialist weapons in mind.

1 Mecha guns start with cylindrical shapes like these, which can be put together to create a gun. Think about how the mecha will hold this weapon – is it wrist-mounted, shoulder-mounted or hand-held? How the gun is fired will determine the elements that you need to include. If it's mounted, it is likely that it won't need a trigger, and if it's hand-held, it will need both a grip and a trigger.

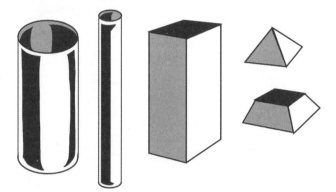

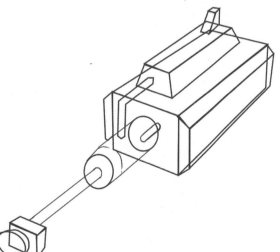

2 Put the block shapes together to get a basic gun shape. Block out the details of the gun with additional cubes and cylinders to make a unique-looking weapon for your mecha.

3 Finish the gun by adding colour that works with the look of your robot character.

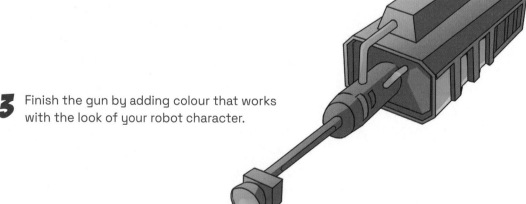

OTHER WEAPONS

Mecha sometimes use hand-held weapons (also called melée weapons). You can refer back to the fantasy weapons shown on pages 34–35, but make them larger and stronger-looking.

1 Think about futuristic weapons for mecha characters. Start with some blocky shapes.

2 Add to these shapes to make a sword or dagger. Mecha need strong, bulky weapons, so get creative with big, blocky designs.

3 Add some colour to complete the weapon.

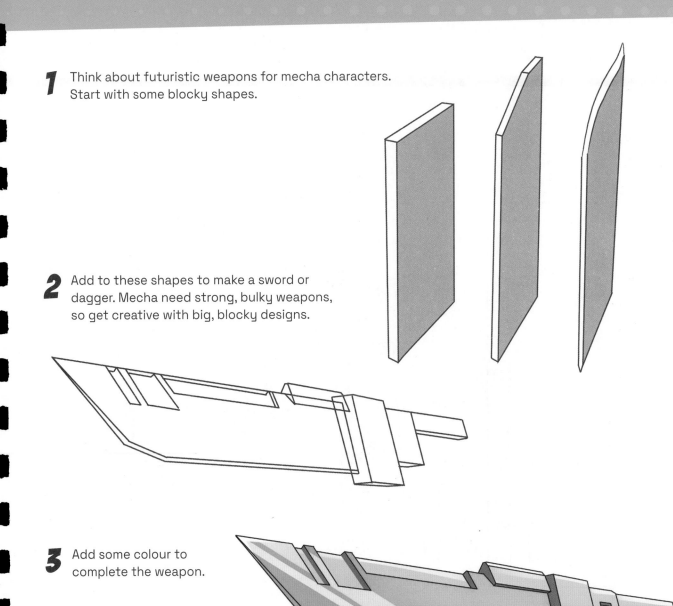

SENSE OF PERSPECTIVE

Now you've drawn your mechas, you need to make them look BIG! You can do this by using sight lines and perspective to give the impression of their sheer size and weight.

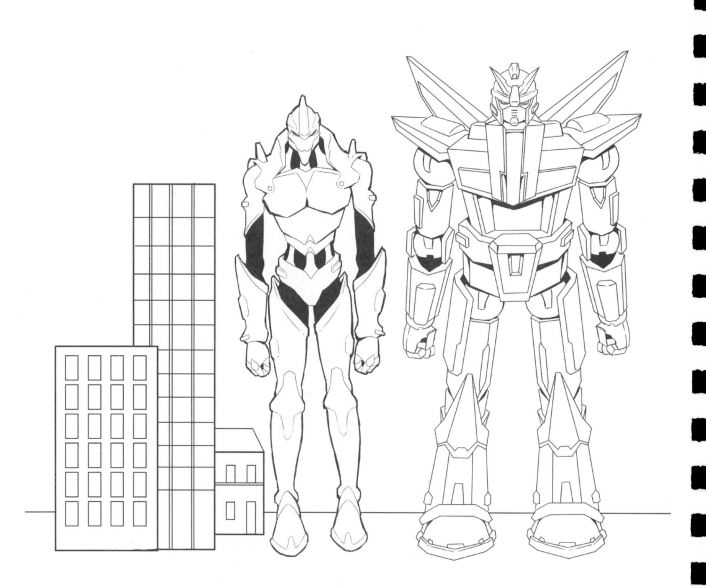

1 Firstly, establish the size of your mecha. Drawing its height in relation to a building can help you to place it in a 3D world. Use 2-point perspective (see pages 26-27) to draw a building that the viewer knows is tall, such as a skyscraper.

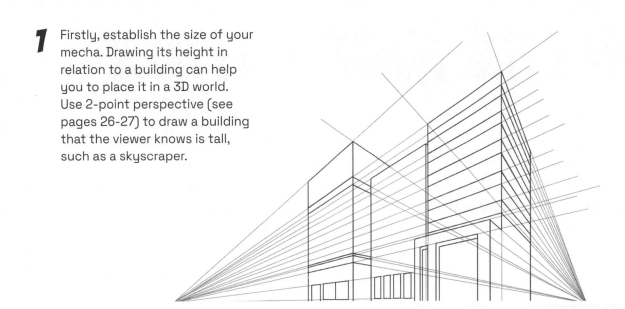

2 Add your mecha to the scene, making sure that it is larger than the building.

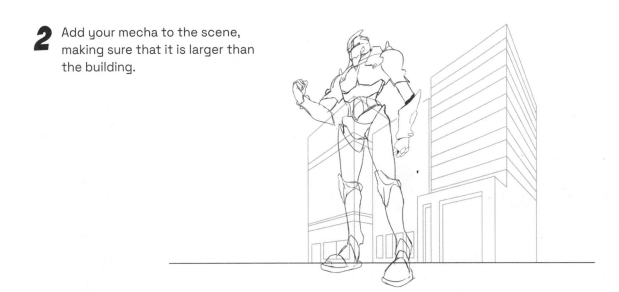

3 When you're happy with the composition, you can lineart the scene and then erase the guidelines.

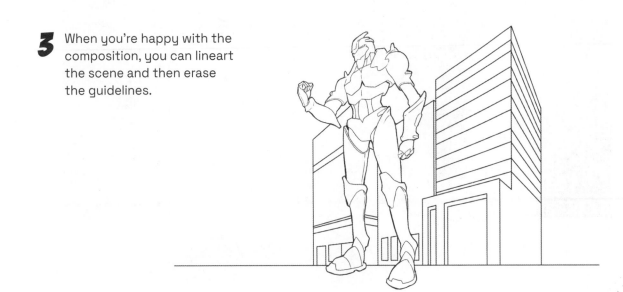

MECHA INSPIRATION

Now you've designed and drawn your own mechas, it's time to explore further. Find inspiration in books, on screen and online and let your imagination take over. Here is a menacing mecha within a futuristic environment. Perhaps you can use this as a starting point for your own designs.

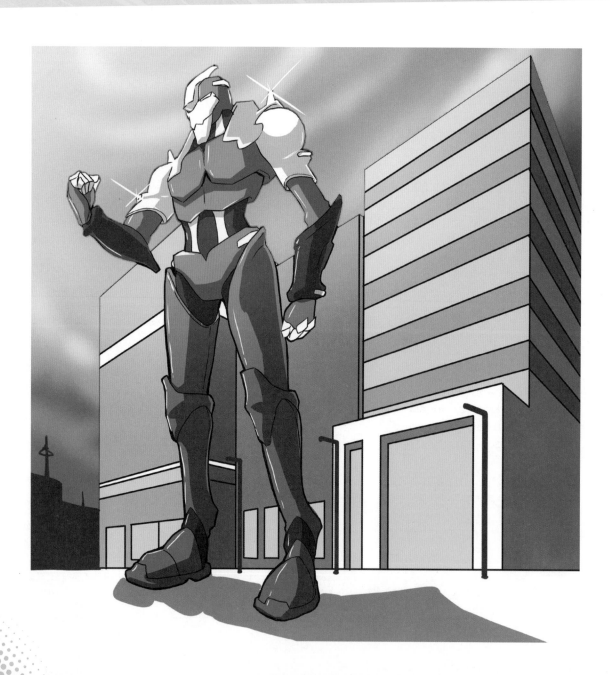

MAKING MANGA

MAKING MANGA

Now that you have mastered a wide range of manga-drawing skills, it's time to take the next step in your manga journey – illustrating a story! In this chapter you'll find out about different styles of manga and discover how they can be used in the context of a story.

SHOUNEN STYLE

Shounen manga (meaning young boys' manga) is a genre of Japanese comics and animated films aimed primarily at a young male audience, typically characterised by action-filled plots. Examples of this genre include *Dragonball Z*, *My Hero Academia* and *Naruto*. If your story fits this style, check out these titles for inspiration.

Shounen style typically has energetic storylines with fast-paced action scenes that revolve around martial arts, fighting or other strongly masculine themes. Here are a few examples of some character types that you could draw for a shounen story.

Panda Boy is a typical shounen character with a muscular physique.

A female genie character ready to fight.

A fantasy shounen-style character with four arms bearing weapons.

SHOUJO STYLE

Shoujo manga (translated as young girls' manga) is a genre of Japanese comics and animated films aimed primarily at a young female audience. It typically focuses on personal and romantic relationships. Examples of this genre are *Sailor Moon*, *Cardcaptor Sakura* and *Magical Madoka*.

This style is heavily romanticised, with an emphasis on feminine designs and stories. That doesn't mean there isn't any action, but there is a focus on the emotional part of the tales. Romance is a key feature in many shoujo manga. Slice-of-life romances and dramas are typical storylines, so consider this genre if you want to focus on the emotional sides of characters. Here are some ideas for the kind of characters that would work for shoujo.

A little queen character ready for fun adventures.

An apprentice sorcerer could be the heroine of your story.

This young girl's brightly coloured hair and clothing is typical in shoujo characters.

A fun character inspired by *Sailor Moon*.

SEINEN STYLE

Seinen manga (translated as youth manga) is a genre of Japanese comics and animated films aimed at teenage and young adult males. Shounen and seinen manga share a lot of similarities, but seinen manga often deals with more mature themes, and is more likely to depict violence in a gratuitous way.

This style is typically gritty and follows mature characters. Examples of this genre include *Gantz*, *Evangelion* and *Berserk*; the stories cover dark themes and are not appropriate for younger readers. If you choose this style, accept that your story will have a more mature angle to it. On these pages are some typical seinen characters.

Two images of a seinen-style cybernetic character. Drawing characters in different poses helps to keep things consistent when you're adding them to your stories.

The twins are waiting
for their sister to bring
the final piece for the
pumpkin ritual in this
dark story.

A fish man.

JOSEI STYLE

Josei manga (translated as women's manga) is a genre of Japanese comics and animated films aimed primarily at mature women. It has a lot in common with the shoujo genre except, as with seinen in relation to shounen, the themes are more mature.

These stories typically revolve around older women and their lives and there is often a real-life drama element within the narrative. Romance also features heavily. Here are some characters that may be found in josei manga.

This girl could be a lead character in a love story.

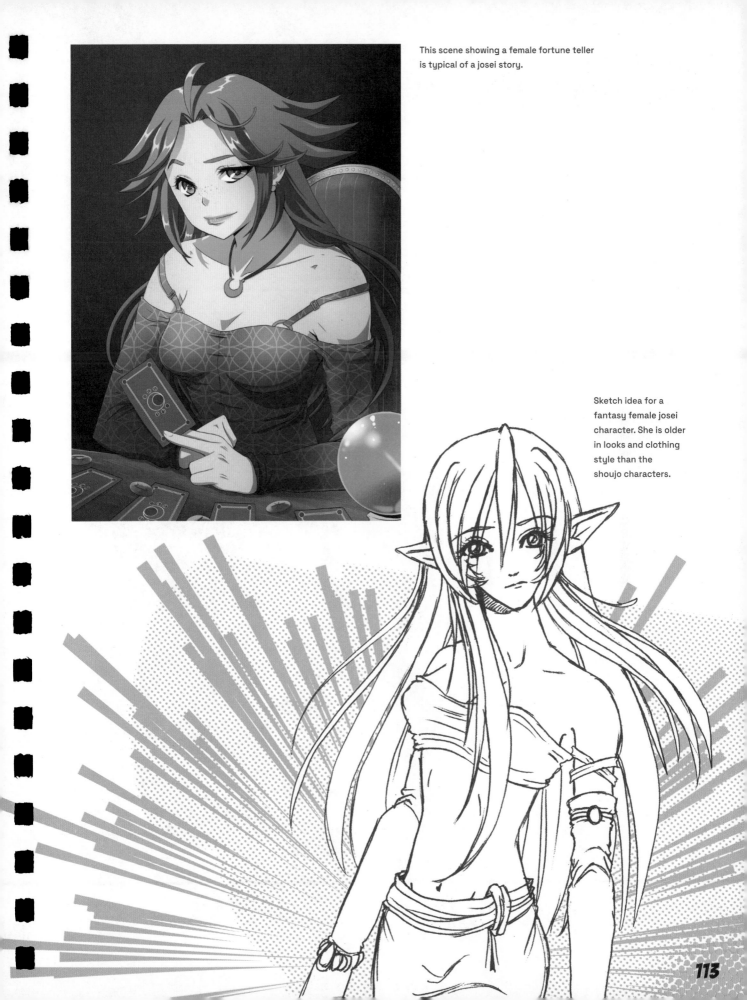

This scene showing a female fortune teller is typical of a josei story.

Sketch idea for a fantasy female josei character. She is older in looks and clothing style than the shoujo characters.

KODOMOMUKE STYLE

Kodomomuke manga (which translates as intended for children) is a genre of Japanese comics and animated films aimed at young children. As you might expect, the stories are usually focused on cute characters and simple stories.

Examples of kodomomuke manga are *Doraemon*, *Pokémon* and *Digimon*. They can be long-running adventure stories or one-offs featuring cute animal mascots. You can easily recognise kodomomuke manga by the bright and vibrant colours. A few kodomuke characters are shown here to give you a feel for this genre.

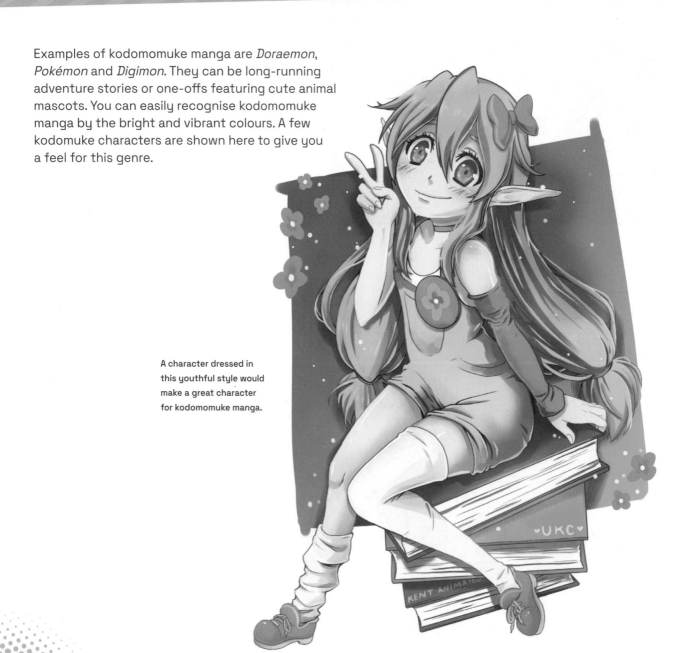

A character dressed in this youthful style would make a great character for kodomomuke manga.

This heart-inspired cat is typical of kodomomuke style with a simple, fun design.

A tiger girl ready for a kodomomuke adventure.

STORY CREATION

Once you have decided on a manga style, you'll need to think about your storyline. Aside from the styles on pages 106–115, there are a few other common genres you might want to consider. Some ideas are given here, although these aren't the only examples you could try. There is plenty of manga out there for inspiration, so the best advice is always to read as much as you can!

ISEKAI MANGA

The quintessential fish-out-of-water story. This is where the main protagonist is flung into an entirely different world from the one they're used to and has to find their way through it to return to their own. This storyline allows for a broad creative approach, as you'll need to design two different worlds!

MAHOU SHOUJO MANGA

A typical storyline for shoujo manga, the mahou shoujo theme is the magical girl genre. This is where the protagonist has the ability to transform into their magical girl persona, and battle evil foes while wearing the cutest of outfits!

SLICE-OF-LIFE MANGA

These stories focus on simple, everyday themes and are great for one-offs if you're interested in writing and drawing comedy.

PAGE LAYOUTS

Traditional Japanese manga pages are read from right to left, which is the opposite of how books are laid out in many other cultures. For these examples, we will be drawing from left to right.

Manga pages are made up of closed and open panels. Closed panels are most commonly used and have lines around them to create enclosed spaces, whereas open panels do not have borders around them. Both these styles are used on each page over the course of a story to keep the pages visually interesting and dynamic.

1 This is a basic manga page layout, with the panels laid out ready for the action to be added. Always leave enough space for speech bubbles. It can be tempting to fill the panels with illustration, only to have to cover up your hard work when you add the speech.

2 Here you can see how those empty panels have been filled, including the closed and open panels and all the speech bubbles. There is quite a bit of planning involved in setting up a page like this, which we will explore on the next page.

USING PANELS

So how do you use panels? How do you know which panels to use, how big to make them, and in what order? To know which panels to use, you need to know what a panel represents: time.

Each panel is a snapshot of time that exists in your manga story, so the size of the panel is directly related to the amount of time spent during that moment. The smaller the panel, the shorter the amount of time being shown; the larger the panel, the longer the amount of time being shown.

A larger panel also allows you to include multiple speech bubbles, allowing for a more natural flow of conversation between two characters. Long, full-page images are great for establishing locations and context.

Here you can see a standard panel.

Speed panels help to create a sense of dynamic motion and urgency. They aren't necessarily rectangular or square and can have unusual angles that fit together. This is a technique commonly used in action scenes.

This page shows how a number of different panel shapes and sizes can work together to give a dynamic feel to your manga stories.

TWO-PAGE LAYOUTS

Sometimes the inclusion of a double spread can add a dynamic feel to your manga. This is where the composition goes over two pages rather than one. You might even have one panel stretch across both pages, with smaller panels to indicate action.

Making a double spread takes more consideration than single pages, as you will have to plan exactly what you want to show and where before you draw. When your manga is in print form, the binding near the spine may obscure some of your image, so remember not to include important elements on this part of the page.

1 Draw the panels you want to use across the two pages. Here the top panel will be used to introduce a scene using a wide shot, and the two lower panels will show that scene in more detail, from two angles.

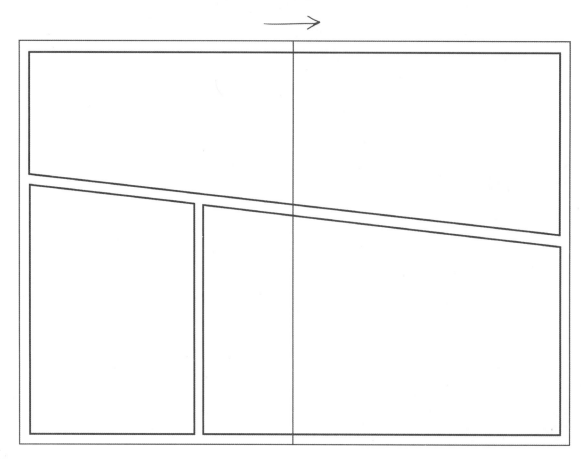

2 With the illustrations added, you can see how the story works across the two pages. This allows a greater level of detail in the establishing shot – more like a panorama – making for a more impactful visual.

Establishing wide shot

Close-up on the girl's face.

A scene from inside the building shown above.

CONVEYING STORY

The next step in creating your own manga story is to make sure you've included all the required elements to tell the tale effectively. Think about the characters you want to include and the elements shown here.

To effectively communicate your story, it's essential that you provide your reader with appropriate context. This means, on every page, you need to answer the following questions:

1. Where and when is this happening?
2. Who is there?
3. What are they doing?

Including the three elements of where, who, and what will help your reader to settle into your story more easily. To make sure you include all these elements, write your script out in full and make sure that you're not going to change any of the words or storyline before you commit even one pencil stroke to paper.

HAVE I THOUGHT ABOUT THE SCRIPT?

When writing a script, always include the following:

- an establishing scene
- a sense of place scene
- a character scene
- dialogue scenes.

By including these scenes, you give your reader key information to convey to them exactly what's going on.

Sense of place panel

Dialogue panel

Character panel

PROCESS OF PAGE CREATION

Now that you have your layout and your script, it's time to put pen to paper. Page creation always starts with a simple thumbnail, which is drawn using your script as a guide. Preparation here is important – knowing what elements will go on each page before you start makes the whole process run more smoothly.

1 Begin by drawing thumbnails for the scenes in your story. Keep these brief and simple and don't forget to leave space for speech bubbles. You can also add simple notes about what will be in each panel. Once you are happy with the pacing of the story and the overall composition, you can start to draw on a full-size page.

2 Now sketch out the contents of the panels. These can also be rough sketches that you add details to later. Make sure that the action in your panels is varied. If there are multiple characters, show them from different angles. The panels can end up looking too similar if you use the same head or body angles for all the characters. You can also change the distance from the viewer to the characters to introduce variety across the panels, and add pop-outs (parts of panels that overlap). This helps direct the viewer where you want them to look.

3 The next stage is to work up the basic sketches into final sketches. Finalise the designs and resolve any elements that you're not happy with. Once done, apply the lineart. Work carefully from left to right across the panels. Use a ruler for the straight lines to keep everything neat. Erase your pencil lines and you are ready to add tone!

ADDING TONE

For many manga stories, tones of grey and black are used instead of full colour. This is because manga was traditionally printed in black and white tones made up of different-sized of dots using lithography printing techniques. Today, a lot of manga is printed digitally. If you are using this method, then you can use grey tones in CMYK to recreate the traditional look.

ADDING TONES DIGITALLY

1 Digitise your lineart image as described on page 69. Using your image software, you should be able to add black and white tones. Some programs have the tones preloaded but you may need to import them in others.

2 Create a new layer below the lineart layer and add tones. Using the lasso tool, select the area you wish to fill with a tone and block it out, creating a solid block of tone. Experiment with the tones and mix them up – remember you'll need to keep your pages consistent, so picking a smaller range of tones to use will make it easier. Toning whole pages is very time consuming!

Higher dot count

Lower dot count

To make things easier for yourself, keep a list of the tones you use for different characters on a reference sheet. This will reduce the time you spend referring back to the tonal values you have used.

ADDING TONES MANUALLY

If you are working using pencil and paper, you can still add tones to your manga. Add the black outlines using an ink pen, then use marker pens to apply black ink over the darker areas and lighter greys for the lighter areas, leaving the very lightest areas white. Traditionally, manga artists would use adhesive transparent screen tones, which can be applied by hand to the paper and then cut out to cover parts of the image to create a look like the one above. As you can see, there is a dotted screen tone effect added to parts of the image.

MANGA COVER DESIGN

A front cover should be an impactful image that will encourage readers to pick up your manga comic! Make sure that it is eye-catching, relevant to the story and interesting.

Think of the cover as a marketing exercise – what is your story about? Who is the main character? How are you going to create an intriguing composition to convey your story to someone at a glance?

A good rule of thumb about covers is to ensure that the main character (or characters) is front and centre. This allows your potential reader to immediately recognise the protagonist throughout the book and gives you a chance to show them in their best light.

Other elements to include are the title and any other information you might need, such as the volume number and logo. As with your pages, make sure you don't spend too much time on details that eventually will be covered up by these elements.

Opposite are two different cover ideas for a story. They both started with a thumbnail, which was worked up into a final design and then coloured. Over the next few pages you'll see this process from start to finish.

LET'S HAVE A THINK ABOUT THE COVER!

CREATING A FRONT COVER

Here we will go through the stages of creating a cover design from thumbnail to finished lineart. You'll want to include the key elements of your lead character and show the style of the manga that you're drawing so that your readers know the genre of story you're telling.

1 Try out some thumbnails. Once you're happy with your design, work up the idea you like the most. Enlarge and start to sketch out more of the composition, adding any elements that you feel are important to the story. Remember to leave space for your title and other features of the cover!

2 When the sketch is complete, finalise the shapes and add the final details. This is also the time to add elements such as the title, the author's name and a logo.

3 Lineart the image with a fineliner, wait for it to dry and erase any pencil marks.

FINISHING TOUCHES

Now let's add the final touches! It's time to add the colour, shadows and all the last details to make your design stand out.

1 If you're working manually, add the colours using marker pens (see page 68). Or you can digitise your image and use a design program to add the flat colours to a new layer underneath the lineart (see pages 68–69). If you intend to print, ensure that the file is in CMYK.

2 If you're working with pen and paper, add the shadows using a black marker. To place the shadows digitally, add a layer over the top of your flat colours and block out the shadows. Use a dark navy colour rather than black – this will help you avoid washing out the shadows on your front cover! Set the opacity of the shadows to about 60% to complete this step. The final step is to add highlights, as described on page 68.

READY, SET, DRAW

READY, SET, DRAW

It's time to put your skills to the test! These pages are for all your wonderful manga drawings.

Time for some action! Sketch your characters in motion.

Use this page to try drawing some different expressions.

Use this page to come up with a background for your own manga story.

Sketch out some ideas for a fantasy manga character here.

Use this page to draw a fantasy creature like a dragon or a centaur.

Use this page to have a go at designing your own mecha!

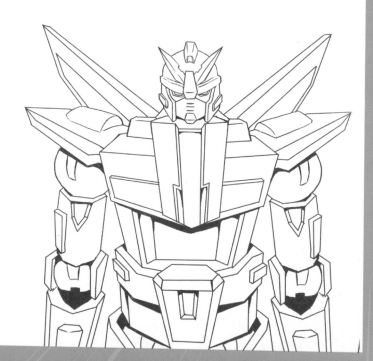

Have a go at creating an original manga cover, featuring your own characters and logo!